Mysterious
Minnesota

ABOUT THE AUTHOR

Adrian Lee (Sauk Centre, Minnesota) was born and grew up in London, England, before traveling extensively throughout Europe, the United States, and other parts of the world. He graduated with a degree from Kent University in 1992 and attended London University from 1996.

Adrian is the president of the Sauk Centre Area Historical Society in Minnesota, the co-founder of The International Paranormal Society, and a member of the Luton Paranormal Society in England. He has investigated ghosts not only in Minnesota but also throughout Britain and the United States—particularly in other Midwestern locations. He is the founder and lead article writer for *Ecto Magazine*, a publication specifically for paranormal investigators, and writes regular columns on Minnesota history for several local newspapers. Adrian is also a qualified Reiki healer and psychic medium, and an experienced Tarot-card reader.

For two years he was the national and international news correspondent and co-host of *Darkness Radio* on KTLK-FM in Minneapolis.

Adrian has also written the book *Tales from a Pioneer Town: The Earliest Stories of Sauk Centre.*

You are welcome to contact Adrian Lee for a psychic reading, to ask about a possible investigation, or if you have any questions. His e-mail address is mysteriousminnesota @yahoo.com, or you can reach him through the website www.heavenandearthessentials.com.

Mysterious Minnesota

Digging Up the Ghostly Past
at
13 Haunted Sites

ADRIAN LEE

Llewellyn Publications
Woodbury, Minnesota

FIRST EDITION
First Printing, 2012

Book design by Donna Burch
Cover design by Ellen Lawson
Cover photo of Chase on the Lake, Walker, Minnesota ©Adrian Lee
Interior photographs provided by Adrian Lee, except for those on the following pages, all of which are reprinted with permission: pp. 39, 40 (by Ron Jamiolkowski), 58, 65, second photo on 129, 136, 203, 229 (by Ron Jamiolkowski), 236 (by A. Anderson), second photo on 247, 259, and 272. The historical photos are courtesy of the Sauk Centre Historical Society.

Llewellyn Publications is a registered trademark of Llewellyn Worldwide Ltd.

Library of Congress Cataloging-in-Publication Data
Lee, Adrian, 1970–
  Mysterious Minnesota : digging up the ghostly past at 13 haunted sites / Adrian Lee. — 1st ed.
    p. cm.
  Includes bibliographical references.
  ISBN 978-0-7387-3149-0
  1. Haunted places–Minnesota. I. Title.
  BF1472.U6L435 2012
  133.109776—dc23
                        2012010692

Llewellyn Worldwide Ltd. does not participate in, endorse, or have any authority or responsibility concerning private business transactions between our authors and the public.
  All mail addressed to the author is forwarded but the publisher cannot, unless specifically instructed by the author, give out an address or phone number.
  Any Internet references contained in this work are current at publication time, but the publisher cannot guarantee that a specific location will continue to be maintained. Please refer to the publisher's website for links to authors' websites and other sources.

Llewellyn Publications
A Division of Llewellyn Worldwide Ltd.
2143 Wooddale Drive
Woodbury, MN 55125-2989
www.llewellyn.com

Printed in the United States of America

DEDICATION

I wish to dedicate this book to my mother—her drawings of small tortoises on my birthday cards are a source of constant annual entertainment; my father, who spent the majority of his Sunday mornings standing in the rain (blown in from the Thames Estuary) watching me chase a football around; and my sister Joanne, whom I fondly recall daily, due to the scars I collected from her during my youth via attacks with golf clubs, hockey sticks, and random electrocutions (during our childhood scrapes and tomfoolery). And finally Lisa, whom I love as the only person I know who goes fishing with a Prada handbag and Gucci shoes.

Full fathom five thy father lies;
Of his bones are coral made;
Those are pearls that were his eyes,
Nothing of him that doth fade,
But doth suffer a sea-change
Into something rich and strange.

—Ariel's song in William Shakespeare's
The Tempest (act I, scene II)

CONTENTS

Where humanity leaves its footprints, paranormal activity will follow.

Introduction

Minnesota has a rich history that stretches back beyond the early European settlers and Native Americans to the Ice Age—much of it long forgotten. It is a history that is interwoven with cultural clashes, conflicts, lawlessness, pioneering spirit, industrialization, economic growth—and, ultimately, death. These events have been played out in Minnesota's antediluvian hotels, gloriously decorated theaters, celebrated towns, forts, fields, and monolithic factories (that now stand idle along the banks of the Mississippi River); these locations can be researched both historically and paranormally to reveal a unique insight into the social history of Minnesota.

The main problem with writing about any historical period is that we weren't actually there—so the research must be as comprehensive as possible to help inform our version and understanding of the events that transpired. This is achieved through the use of primary source material: newspaper articles, period documents, letters, photographs, banking details, and firsthand interviews. To these resources I added the evidence of scientific paranormal investigations—incidents of murder, fatal accidents, illness, executions, and military engagements have left a layer of paranormal activity that can be documented; these can then be placed into the context of the newly found historical facts for verification. I don't just want to write about history; I want to experience it.

ABOUT ME

I was born and grew up in London, England, before traveling extensively throughout Europe, America, and the rest of the world. I graduated with a degree from Kent University in 1992 and attended London University from 1996; I studied art history and history methodologies for my Master's degree, and more recently I studied religious humanities. I taught for thirteen years in London and the English counties of Northamptonshire, Buckinghamshire, and Bedfordshire—becoming the head of several history and art departments and a local education authority advisor. I currently lecture on all aspects of the paranormal—including UFOs and angels.

I am the co-founder of The International Paranormal Society and a member of the Luton Paranormal Society in England; I have comprehensively investigated ghosts and paranormal activity in Britain, Europe, and America—particularly in the Midwest. I first became interested in the paranormal after experiencing several events in my childhood home; progressively throughout my adult life the idea of interfacing with the dead became intriguing to me from a historical perspective (what could be more exciting for a historian than to interview someone who died 200 years ago?).

I have always believed in ghosts, and I think British people generally have a more open outlook towards paranormal phenomena; this thinking is imparted by the amount of history that surrounds us on a daily basis and the heritage of ghost stories that are familiar within our nation. The concept of energy and spirits has also seeped into our cultural psyche from the thousands of years of pagan philosophies and worship (archaeologists believe that Stonehenge was erected around 2500 BCE) that have assimilated themselves into our modern-day religious and festive conventions.

I first came to Minnesota early in 2008 to investigate and work on several paranormal video productions. I then spent two years working in Minneapolis as the national and international news correspondent for a live paranormal talk radio show on KTLK-FM. During this time I also created, and worked as the lead writer for, a quarterly publication specifically aimed at paranormal investigators. I am the current president of the Sauk Centre Area Historical Society, and I write regular history columns for the Sauk Centre Herald and several other local newspapers.

My paranormal investigations are informed by my clairvoyance—I see very detailed and specific pictures presented to me by the deceased, which allow me to have a very precise communication with the spirits. I also have remote-viewing skills and clairsentience (I use these abilities effectively for my Tarot-card readings and Reiki healing work). My psychic sensitivities were dormant for a long period in my youth, with only occasional glimpses of what could be achieved. It was through the process of working with other sensitives and being exposed to all manner of paranormal contact (coupled with my own personal psychic development) that my skills improved, and I am now in a position in which I can access and utilize them freely. Like any other ability, my clairvoyance continues to evolve and become stronger—through the implementing of structures surrounding my design for life, critical introspection, and practice.

THE TEAM

The International Paranormal Society is a nonprofit worldwide organization created to research, investigate, analyze, and document anomalous events that fall outside the realm of conventional scientific research. Our primary areas of interest include hauntings, apparitions, poltergeist activity, and psychic phenomena—with a focus on sharing evidence and professional practice for the aim of providing proof for the existence of an afterlife.

The following are core members of The International Paranormal Society in the Midwest; the investigations in this book were undertaken with this team—a further twenty members were used sporadically, depending who was available and the size of the investigation. Each investigator is on the team for the skills and knowledge he or she brings—I trust each one implicitly and feel safer for having them standing by my side.

Lisa is a team leader and was the original founder of the Twin Cities Paranormal Society; she is a psychic sensitive with a wealth of paranormal investigating experience. She is also my wife.

Steve R. is a team leader based in Wisconsin; he is dedicated and brings a down-to-earth, calm, reliable, grounded nature to investigations; he originally contacted me and asked to join the team.

Steve H. is our theology expert and pastor; he brings his faith and the weight of the Christian church with him. He is based in central Minnesota and is one of my most trusted friends—we originally met at a paranormal event in Stearns County.

Ron is based in Chicago and is a highly experienced investigator. Having investigated all over the United States, he is our technical expert and belongs to several other competent teams in the Midwest. We originally met on the Internet and then in person at a paranormal event.

Lou lives in St. Paul and is originally from South Africa. She is a very committed investigator.

Heather and Ashley are sisters and live in southwestern Minnesota; they are both in the process of developing their psychic abilities. We met by chance at the Palmer House Hotel.

Angela originally investigated throughout the Midwest with Steve R.—she is a member of the U.S. Army.

Mary brings a wealth of knowledge, having investigated extensively throughout the U.S. She lives near Duluth (and we tease her that she is practically Canadian).

Warren is an enthusiastic investigator who has run several teams of his own. I originally met Warren at the Mounds Theatre—where he was giving paranormal tours.

Kate is new to paranormal investigating and brings an enthusiasm and a thirst for knowledge.

Tim Baxton is a well-known and respected psychic medium based in Duluth.

EQUIPMENT

Here is a brief description of the equipment I use throughout this book:

The ghost box is a radio receiver that continually scans both AM and FM frequencies on a loop—not stopping on any particular station. It generates both white noise and small one-word snippets as it rolls rapidly past each station. It is believed that entities can access the words that are being spoken and form them into responses—like a speaking electronic Ouija board. This is similar to a ransom note, where individual letters or words might be pieced together from various newspaper headlines to form a sentence. It is possible to have a dialogue where every word in the sentence is from a different source, with varying accents and gender. Communication is also achieved by hearing voices coming through over the top of the white noise, as the device scans between the broadcasting frequencies. It is theorized that entities have trouble articulating due to their lack of vocal cords; it is believed this device can provide a vehicle for that communication.

The Ovilus is a tool that detects changes in temperature and electromagnetic fields (EMF) to operate a computer with a lexicon of words and phonetics programmed into it—so a spirit can communicate by making subtle changes to the atmosphere. It is believed that an entity, with practice, can facilitate ambient environmental changes to choose the words it requires to communicate. Interestingly, some of the words I am now starting to hear from this device have not been programmed into the machine.

A digital voice recorder (DVR) is used to record results obtained from the ghost box and the Ovilus. DVRs can also record voices, believed to be from spirits, in a stimulus and response situation; this is due to the DVR's sensitivity to sounds and frequencies. These spirit responses are referred to as electronic voice phenomena (EVPs) and are rarely heard in real time.

Electromagnetic field (EMF) meters are used to detect electromagnetic energy; it is believed that entities require energy to manifest or to be physical—which can then be measured. When electricity flows, it sends electrons through wires or a space, generating a corresponding perpendicular magnetic field that emanates around the electrical flow into the area around it—which can be measured in *milligauss*. To give you an indication of the strength of these readings, the magnetic field generated by the transformer in a cordless phone or clock radio can be up to 1,000 milligauss, but this dissipates to around three to four milligauss from a distance of around twelve inches. It is important to remember that transformers with a magnetic field can also be found in cell phone chargers, audio systems, electric clocks, and fluorescent bulbs—EMF can also penetrate walls, objects, and humans. Due to the possibility of EMF contaminating our evidence from outside influences like electrical cabling (often hidden behind walls and under floors), I instigate baseline tests before an investigation to ascertain the possibility of EMF pollution. I also ensure that all lighting and electrical devices are turned off (another reason why investigators work in the dark); this includes cell phones, as they will still look intermittently for a signal when they are set on silent, generating a level of EMF.

METHODS

The combination of historical research and paranormal investigating can create a very powerful tool, especially if you can utter the name of a person that was intrinsic to the fabric of a building and has long since been forgotten. In my experience, a spirit cannot resist talking to you when you ask for them by name, a name that may not have been spoken in that environment for well over 150 years; this proved to be a surprisingly useful tool and acted as a great catalyst for making a connection.

My success at making regular contact with the deceased was also facilitated by my explanation of what I was doing and why I was there; I asked them how to spell their names and if my research and details were correct—under those circumstances many wanted then to engage with me and my team. Other stimuli I employed had to do with the ways in which I tried to keep the conversation flowing. For example, if the entity said his name was "William," I would respond by saying, "Do you prefer being called William or Bill? I just want to get it right." At that point the entity would respond with his name again for clarification—making my evidence stronger by removing the element of randomness (without directly asking the entity to repeat the name for me).

Interestingly, this dialogue became a two-way process over time, in that the ghosts and spirits provided me with information about which I was previously unaware. I would not take anything I was told from the other side at face value of course, but when armed with a new date, detail, or name to research, I found the information offered to be true. I cannot explain how this process works outside of being paranormal phenomena, but it does. This supplemented my research and gave me specific data that focused my resources to good effect and led me into areas I would not have otherwise explored, revealing more than I would have found through traditional nonparanormal means alone.

The locations described in this book are haunted by multiple entities that are there to be engaged with—many of which I have researched over a number of years through countless investigations. They remain present because some feel they still have jobs to do out of obligation; some have messages to give; some have unfinished work to do; and others are just curious and like frequenting a building they loved when they were alive. They actively want you to document their names and achievements. Because those details have been lost to the knowledge of humanity, this process then strengthens the concept that ghosts are here to remind us of our past; and as any historian will tell you, we can only judge the past by what is left to us in the present.

Everything paranormal I have documented is 100 percent fact; as a qualified practicing historian and experienced and respected paranormal investigator, it would not be beneficial for my reputation to elaborate upon anything other than the facts. In actuality, such a wealth of paranormal evidence presented itself that I had the difficult task of editing down my findings into chapter-sized texts—I could have written an entire book on the Palmer House Hotel alone—so there would be no reason to add details that are untrue.

All of the paranormal phenomena I have documented throughout this book were witnessed by the professional and experienced members of The International Paranormal Society who assisted me in my investigations. This evidence also exists as video footage, photographs, documented measurable data, and audio files captured on numerous occasions by multiple recordings of the same incident. I have also used a number of trusted and proven psychics as a vehicle to provide a thorough investigative experience. Interestingly, the names, dates, and information they gave me throughout the investigations were previously unknown and were then uncovered retrospectively by myself.

On this journey I have spoken with entities, been touched, seen apparitions, and witnessed events that I cannot rationally explain—so by default they are paranormal (above and beyond normality), but they are all documented here for you to form your own opinions. Some of the ghosts and spirits are good and some are bad; this is just a reflection of society in general, but in all circumstances respect was shown to those I encountered. Our investigations are not about provoking innocent, kind deceased people into performing parlor tricks; they are about recording their lives and thoughts to give us a better understanding of the history of the state of Minnesota.

My hope is that this book goes some way to increasing the profile and importance of many of the sites I have investigated, helping to diminish the continuing threat many of them face from redevelopment—so that both we and the ghosts can carry on enjoying them and frequenting them in the years to come.

CHAPTER 1

Minneapolis City Hall

MINNEAPOLIS

The spirit of the hanging judge, ghostly criminals, and a creepy haunted elevator mean the only people spending the night at City Hall are doing so under lock and key.

Minneapolis City Hall is such an impressive building, inside and out; it has all the architectural features you would expect to find on a stereotypical haunted property. I explored the building extensively on a single day with a relatively small team and managed to access the most paranormally active locations with help from our guide. The very nature of the building and the headlines it created, from the executions and events that took place there, meant I could easily find and research large amounts of historical information; these sources included obituaries, articles from period newspapers (both online and from the Minnesota Historical Society), and facts provided to me by City Hall employees.

HISTORY

The evolution of the Minneapolis skyline during the mid-to-late nineteenth century was determined by the city's growth in population and economics—which is reflected in the construction of City Hall. The lack of available space at the original Hennepin County and Minneapolis government office buildings decreed that a new site was required. Many of the quickly erected and technically poor buildings of the pioneer days found themselves being replaced at this time, as they were not thought befitting of a burgeoning state wanting to embrace modernity. They were also becoming unsafe with age.

The Minneapolis-based architects Long and Kees were employed to design the building and oversee the construction. Franklin B. Long and Frederick Kees were responsible for much of the city's distinctive look during the company's twelve-year existence. Most of these buildings have been torn down, but Long and Kees' work can still be seen in the Lumber Exchange Building (1885), the Hennepin Center for the Arts (1888, originally built as a Masonic Temple), and the Flour Exchange Building (1892).

Long and Kees had a history of designing and constructing churches across the Midwest, and they applied this knowledge to create the grandeur and status of the Minneapolis City Hall—providing a lasting public monument befitting justice, lawmaking, and city governance. This was achieved through using the religious semiotics of Romanesque architecture, combined with the revival Richardsonian

The rotunda of Minneapolis City Hall

style. The design had clearly defined forms in regular symmetrical planes, sturdy piers, curved arches, and embedded conical-capped cylindrical towers. Its bold, blank stretches of thick walling, with decorative arcading, contrasted brilliantly with the bands of narrow windows.

Before building work could commence, the Washington School (the first schoolhouse in Minneapolis west of the Mississippi) had to be demolished and cleared, along with an entire city block of 680,000 square feet; the groundbreaking took place in 1889. Ortonville granite was used in the construction; it was transported with some difficulty from the quarries of Big Stone County at the western tip of Minnesota next to the South Dakota border—many of the blocks weighed over twenty tons. The original design only used granite to provide strength in the foundations, but the look was so striking that public support championed the construction of the whole building in this medium, replacing the original brickwork design for the upper stories. This gave the building its famous reddish-brown appearance.

The unexpected use of granite significantly tripled the construction cost for the building; the original cost was expected to be $1,150,000. By the time the interior paintwork had finished drying and the final piece of carpet had been laid, it had risen to $3,554,000—at twenty-eight cents per cubic foot. The original roof was installed in matching red terra cotta tiles but did not stand up to the rigors of a Minnesota winter, so had to be replaced. The current copper roof was then fitted and soon became weathered, complementing the color of the granite walls perfectly with its verdigris hue. The roof weighs 180,000 pounds and was believed to be the biggest copper roof anywhere in the country when it was installed—its current scrap market value would be around $550,000. City Hall was not officially finished until 1909 (nine years after Long and Kees had ceased to exist)—although Hennepin County employees started to occupy the building in 1895 on the finished 4th Avenue side; the 3rd Avenue site was occupied from 1906 onwards.

Minneapolis City Hall was the first government building to have its floors supported from the courtyard's internal and external walls, independently of partitions. This allowed future generations to add or remove internal walls without compromising the structural strength of the building, rendering some of the internal walls over five feet thick. Bedford limestone was transported by rail from Indiana for interior use—it is most noticeable in the rotunda, a large five-story feature on the 4th Street side of the building. In 1906 the American artist Larkin Goldsmith Mead created the *Father of Waters* sculpture that sits prominently in the rotunda. It is carved from famous Carrara marble quarried in Tuscany—the building material of ancient Rome and the medium of the Renaissance sculptors. Good luck is believed to come to all those who touch the toes of this large neoclassical sculpture—I did this before I started exploring the darker recesses of the building.

THE HANGING OF JOHN MOSHIK

Investigating City Hall is like wandering around a cold, reverential cathedral. Its stone floors are swathed in a kaleidoscope of reflected stained glass. It shimmers with each flickering of an outside street lamp, echoing your every step—even those belonging to ones who have passed on. The sound of a dropped flashlight would send a careering cacophony of noise crashing through the concourse. The fifth floor is where the rumors and stories of paranormal activity abound—it is believed the ghost of John Moshik haunts this area. The tales of full-bodied apparitions, ice-cold unexplained winds whistling down walkways, and eerie footsteps are recounted by the lawyers and judges who have experienced these events.

In March 1898 John Moshik was hanged to death inside City Hall, the last person to be executed in Hennepin County. He was placed on trial in the Chapel Courtroom for a murder he committed during a bungled robbery—which netted him just $14. Moshik pleaded "inherited insanity" for the crime but was found guilty and sentenced to hang by the neck until dead. The gallows were erected on the fifth floor next to the death room above what is now the laundry and staff dining area. Moshik's hands and feet were bound, and he was positioned under the gallows. The noose was placed around his neck and tightened in readiness. The clock twitched slowly to the allocated time, and under a murmur of praying the trap door beneath Moshik was released—suspending him by the neck. Later that same day the front page of the *St. Paul Daily Globe* described the events that led up to the execution:

> John Moshik pays the penalty for murder—John Moshik was hanged in the Hennepin county jail, Minneapolis, at 3.34 a.m. With his life he paid the price for the murder of John Lemke. At 3 o'clock this morning preparations for the execution were begun, and a few minutes later Moshik was led into the room

for his execution. He was accompanied by a deputy sheriff and a jailer. He exhibited no signs of weakness and walked up the steps to the scaffold with a firm step. He was placed on the trap and asked by the sheriff if he had anything he wished to say. "I have not," was his reply, and these were his last words. His feet were then tied and the cap drawn over his face. Sheriff Phillips himself sprang the trap. As the body dropped the cap fell off Moshik's head. It was quickly picked up by one of the deputies and replaced over the dying man's face. The glimpse of his face did not show any signs of suffering and it was then supposed his neck was broken by the fall. This was later found to be the case when the body was cut down, fifteen minutes after the drop and fall. Moshik's was an execution devoid of the cheap heroics that have marked the last hours of criminals who have met violent death at the hands of the law, but whose lives or crimes were out of the ordinary. His death scarce caused a tremor in the community outside a small home circle in St. Paul. There was nothing in the man or his crime to attract the attention of the learned or curious.

The proximity of his death brought the fear of it to the murderer yesterday morning. He had lost his flippant humor—it had been vulgarly, profanely flippant before. He was shaved and washed in his old quarters and a complete suit of clothes furnished him. And he admired himself greatly in spite of the fact that he knew he was dressed for the gallows. When he was dressed he received the ministrations of his church.

Then he breakfasted heartily and settled down for his last day after being transferred to a new cell in the insane ward.

The hanging took place in the presence of a turbulent mob of men, who for hours had clamored and screamed and fought for a place.[1]

The whole affair from start to finish had been badly managed; it was suggested that Sheriff Phillips was to blame, for he was inexperienced in such matters (but there were no men employed as journeymen executioners who could have done the job better). Common sense also appeared to be in short supply, as over 450 men clamored to spectate on the execution. It is possible that fifty had some sort of justifiable excuse for their presence, but for the rest of them the affair appeared to be a high function in low life.

When he had taken his place on the trap he stared straight in front of him, after the first glance upward. His face was set and corpse-like. Nine men out of ten in the room expected a scene, and Moshik had made his mind up to disappoint them. It was all over quickly enough. He was asked if he had anything to say and mumbled, "No." He told them "to pull tighter around the feet," and the flap of Harry Hayward's cap shut out the light from his eyes forever. The priest stepped from in front of him and Sheriff Phillips pulled the lever. The one sign of human feeling exhibited by the mob was in the little wave of horror that distinctly passed over the upturned faces as the cap fell off the head of the hanging man and showed his distorted features.[2]

The only way to ascend to the fifth floor was via a single elevator, which led to a thirty-minute delay in the hanging of Moshik, as the thronged hysterical mob fought in the lobby to get to the gallows. This created such a disturbance that Moshik begged the sheriff to hang him early. To add a bizarre twist to the whole proceedings, a cat had found its way into the building; it positioned itself like a harbinger of doom on the arm of the gallows and observed the madness below. Cats have a long association with the paranormal and hold both a revered and malevolent place in human culture. This dates back to the ancient Egyptians, who worshipped the cat for its powers of fertility and protection. This belief resulted in cats having the freedom to roam unchallenged. In the European folklore of the medieval period, cats became an animal associated with the Devil, and were sent to assist witches in their evil deeds and practices; they were also believed to be one of the animals linked with a witch's ability to shapeshift.

Legend dictates that Moshik's execution was cursed with more than poor crowd control and a mysterious cat. It is believed the noose slipped from Moshik's neck and became caught under his chin—causing him to writhe and choke on his own vomit. It took the guards several minutes to realize that things were not going according to plan, and they eventually brought Moshik down to rearrange the noose; they then tried to hang him for a second time—it took a further three minutes before he died. Whether this legend is true remains to be seen, but nothing was documented in the contemporary press—perhaps due to the moral obligation of censorship not to reveal the macabre and upsetting nature of the hanging.

Certainly the debacle of this execution became the catalyst to lobby against capital punishment in Minnesota. It initially triggered *Smith's Law* in 1889, which became adopted as a half-measure when the death-penalty abolition law was unable to pass. It removed the spectacle of public executions, requiring death sentences to be carried out after midnight behind prison walls. The press called this process the *midnight assassination law*; it was subsequently employed by other states as public executions became defunct.

The abolition of the state death penalty was finally achieved after the hanging of William Williams in 1906. His execution was also so poorly conducted that Williams became the last man to be hanged in Minnesota. Williams (1877–1906) was sexually involved a with a teenager named Johnny Keller. Keller's family intervened to stop their son from continuing the relationship, which sent Williams into a fit of rage, and he coldly shot and killed Keller and his mother in their own home.

Williams was sentenced to death and was hanged on February 13, 1906, in the basement of the Ramsey County Jail. Unfortunately, as the trap door released, his neck stretched by four and one-half inches and the rope by a further eight inches; this meant that his feet touched the ground. Three police officers then rushed to pull the rope higher until Williams died—an unfortunate fourteen minutes later. This debacle instigated the final push that saw the removal of the death penalty in Minnesota in 1911.

INVESTIGATION

The Ghostly Chapel Courtroom

The Chapel Courtroom in Minneapolis City Hall soon started to gain a reputation for being haunted by the ghost of the disgruntled John Moshik. Strange occurrences increased after the 1950s, when the floor was completely remodeled and subdivided into a different layout; it is a common phenomenon when refurbishing or restoring a building that paranormal activity heightens. This is through the workmen creating a large amount of noise and disruption, stirring up entities that were lying dormant and resting peacefully. The fear of change in a familiar and safe environment can also be a catalyst for entities (which try and stop the process from being completed).

Ghosts and spirits can also use the energy given to them by the tools and equipment of the workmen, in what are normally quiet areas. Entities are also capable of attaching themselves to furniture and possessions, like a chair or desk that has been occupied by the same person for many years; this can also be true of ornaments and pictures that have an emotive significance to a deceased worker or inmate. If these articles are moved in preparation for building work or refurbishment, it can create paranormal activity.

In 1978 the fifth floor was acquisitioned and used by the Hennepin County Adult Detention Center to detain sixty to seventy inmates. The floor now provides three separate holding areas, visiting rooms, and a kitchen, dining area, and laundry facility. It did not take long for Moshik's ghost to make its presence known though, and inmates started to complain about seeing a strange man looking back at them from the window of the common room. The staff investigated each event fully but found no evidence to back up the claims. The heavily monitored security video cameras showed no one entering the common room and revealed no sign of an intruder. Activity is not just restricted to the fifth floor, however, as office workers have experienced the sounds of toilets flushing on their own, and the mayor was perplexed at finding rearranged pictures in the mayoral office.

The Clock Tower

At the time of its construction, City Hall claimed to have the world's largest clock tower; its original ten-bell chime was first played on March 10, 1896, and it has continued to be heard every Friday and on Sunday afternoons during the warmer months.

The elevator up to the bell tower is as big as a coffin and just as welcoming, barely able to contain four people comfortably. When I took the elevator, the personal space of the other passengers fully enveloped me. The open-caged door raced past each floor directly in front of my face—health and safety did not appear to be a prerequisite of the nineteenth-century designer, and any unsuspecting finger or protruding body part would have been dispatched with all the ease and efficiency of a sharp pair of scissors. The elevator jumped, creaked, and groaned with random regularity as I shuffled uneasily on the spot like a man standing in a minefield. I distracted myself from the discomfort of the ride by observing the graffiti scratched into the elevator walls dating from the turn of the last century. The word *graffiti* comes from the Italian *graffio*, "scratch," and examples date back to the civilizations of ancient Greece and the Roman Empire—with a heavy dose of irony, we arrived at level thirteen.

I pushed hard against a frozen door that was blocking my path to the roof. It gave and flew open, exposing me to the kind of cold winds that bite into your soul and remove your core body heat. It was the kind of chill that leaves you sitting in a hot bath wondering why you're still shivering and covered in goose bumps. If spirits resided on the roof, they would not be bothered by me. Only investigators lacking claustrophobic tendencies with an unnatural love of heights and a hardy resistance to subzero temperatures would be collecting evidence here—and I do not fall into that Venn diagram.

The Haunted Red Elevator

The team and I then took a second elevator, aptly called the "red elevator," down to the records room; it was the elevator the morbid masses of spectators squeezed into during their bid to see John Moshik's death. It is believed the interior of the elevator was painted red in an attempt to mask the blood splatters that adorned the walls; a stain left from an era of police brutality that saw prisoners beaten away from the public's gaze—the later addition of a surveillance camera put a stop to these alleged misconducts. My journey in this elevator was again filled with apprehension, as I had previously read about the frequency with which it had failed—even when it was new. This article is from *The Saint Paul Globe*, from 1905:

Elevator is stuck—Vags have to walk four flights to jail.

The elevator in the new police station on the top floor of the Minneapolis City Hall went "bump" about 11 o'clock last night and as a result the bums and vags had to be walked up four flights of stairs. The drunks that could not walk were carried by the husky attendant of the patrol wagon, Peter McLaughlin, who, after he had carried an inebriate of about 239 pounds up the stairs, struck and declared he would organize a labor union. The elevator is hitched somewhere near the top floor of the building. The attendant said it is "stuck" and there are many persons who will agree with him. The old station, which was abandoned the latter part of last week, was utilized for a portion of the night.[3]

The large square records room is surrounded, from floor to ceiling, in three tiered levels of shelving; this depository is home to the oldest collection of Minnesota law books and directories. Lisa reported a feeling of apprehension as she reached the original iron stairs that allowed access to the highest parts—she was eager to come back down again. This was a paranormally quiet area, reflective of the library feel of the atmosphere—but I did note several cold drafts of air blowing against me. There seemed no obvious reason for this experience; the room has air-tight shuttered windows and there appeared no other way a chilling breeze could travel through the room.

The Oppressive Third Floor

I made my way to the third floor—a collection of long shadows thrown against vast, empty, soulless corridors devoid of interest, which portray a feeling of foreboding and melancholy, like an Edward Hopper painting. I walked along the expansive stretch of Romanesque mosaic flooring, with each crack acknowledged as a point of interest for a wondering mind starved of visual stimuli. I spent a short while setting up trigger objects along the corridor, hoping that a poltergeist might be able to move or interfere with them in our absence. Trigger objects can be varied in their deployment. I have used toys, crucifixes, playing cards, shotglasses, and even fishing bobbers. On this occasion I placed three pieces of paper on the floor at various intervals and drew around a coin (a quarter) on each one, so if the coin became displaced I would know. I photographed the experiments to keep a further record of their starting positions.

The air felt heavy and intense. Team member Lou complained that her skull felt as though it were being crushed under the pressure. At this point Lisa started feeling a tingle in the top of her scalp and said that she felt the presence of spirits; we all stood there sickened by the dense, nauseating miasma.

Air pressure is the weight exerted by the air around us, which is directly related to its temperature and altitude. It has been determined that even the smallest changes in pressure can affect us physically; the nerve endings on our joints have receptors that can sense pressure changes. Headaches can occur and even the regularity of births and sperm counts

The haunted third floor of Minneapolis City Hall

can be altered noticeably. These physical changes are so subtle that our brains may not be consciously recognizing the shifts in our bodily functions—but we may still pick up an unconscious sense that something is happening.

Changes in barometric pressure directly affect the amount of oxygen in our body—higher pressure will generate more oxygen than lower pressure. The blood vessels in our brain contract and expand to regulate the amount of blood flow required in any given area, to compensate for the variation in oxygen levels. This regulatory process and subsequent change of blood flow can result in neuropathic pain—this can vary from a mild headache to more intense pressure headaches or migraines. Anti-inflammatory pain-relief drugs work by reducing the inflammation of the blood vessels. The human body also feels the weight of the air and begins to experience problems with mobility; joints are especially vulnerable to these pressure changes when the fluid surrounding the joint becomes inflamed.

It is possible that paranormal activity can trigger changes in atmospheric pressure; it is my experience that you can sense when activity is imminent, due to noticeable changes in the atmosphere a minute or two before the incident takes place. This would suggest that paranormal activity causes air pressure to change, or that naturally occurring changes in pressure encourage and facilitate paranormal activity. Paranormal activity could create a pressure change if its arrival provides a significant temperature drop, as reported by the phenomenon of cold spots. A sharp drop in temperature would create high pressure, causing an increase of ions—often associated with paranormal activity (there is a shift in the ratio of positive and negative ions in the air during a thunderstorm).

If hot air rises and cold, denser air (coming from the roof) wants to sink, it would be reasonable to believe that the two would meet at some given point in the building. If that point happens to be the fifth floor, for example, then the meeting of the two pressures would create a micro-atmosphere—which would generate moisture and ions (perfect conditions for ghosts and spirits). Entities may then harness the static energy available to them in the air, in the same way they vampirically drain my batteries and power supplies. In old buildings with less climate control, pockets of perfect conditions could be created in various positions throughout the interior—by the meeting of low and high pressure (this may explain why newer buildings appear less active). These pressure differences then create a physical change in our chemistry that becomes the source of headaches and discomfort—something that has been labeled as paranormal, but could in fact be the by-product of a perfect catalytic atmosphere. It could therefore be suggested that certain floors or rooms in buildings that are labeled paranormally active just happen to be the areas where perfect conditions are created.

Lisa claimed that she felt a strong criminal presence within the corridors of the third floor; she believed that spirits with ill intent were lurking in the shadows and observing our movements—ready to pounce if an opportunity arose to undertake a crime. It is possible that spirits with a criminal past would want to reside in the darkest, most remote areas of the building, due to fear of interacting with the legal system—it is never prudent to make yourself noticeable to those who uphold the law if you have something to hide. I thought it seemed unlikely that criminal activity would be prevalent in such a stronghold of justice and law, so I researched to see if crimes had taken place within the building. To my surprise I discovered an article from 1904 outlining such an event:

> The Unprofessional Crook—A thief, a big burly criminal with a slanting forehead and prognathous jaw, attempted a hold-up in the corridor of the Minneapolis City Hall Saturday. He attacked the young woman and was only beaten off because the victim had been employed about the building for some time and was prepared to repel boarders. The incident calls attention to the commendable pluck of the young woman, who operates the cigar stand. At the same time it invites particular notice to what may be termed the unprofessionalism of the Minneapolis crook.[4]

The journalist clearly believes that a breakdown within the normal framework of Minnesota society occurs when a criminal starts going about his business in an unprofessional manner—suggesting that we should strive to be robbed as professionally as possible. One almost has to admire the unwavering fortitude of a criminal who decides to conduct such a blunt and blatant criminal action in a courthouse. I did discover that the interior of City Hall was used at one time, early in its inception, as an indoor mall—with fruit stands and small shops selling their wares; this was due to the spiraling construction costs and was implemented as a way of raising capital to finish the building work. The criminal action does highlight the idea that City Hall was awash with undesirables—frequenting court hearings and providing support for criminal colleagues, friends, and family. It appears that the artistic and decorative surroundings belied a habitat for criminal intent—as Lisa had foretold.

The Spirit of the Hanging Judge

We soon found ourselves outside Room 326, the old office of the so-called "Hanging Judge." The number 326 is perceived to be lucky in Chinese culture, as the number three refers to the minimum number of points required to make a geometric shape—and thus is the starting point for all things. So 326 is looked upon as a reflection of progress and a doubling of all the things you have or started with—as three times two equals six; by this measure Eastern culture embraces 666 as the ultimate lucky number. This office is far from being a lucky room though, especially for those individuals who experienced the ultimate sharp end of Minnesota justice. We turned the Ovilus on and tried to make contact with those who may have been kept from passing over by a strong sense of injustice. Lisa's words echoed through the corridors as she said, "We're just here to spend some time with you."

"Why?" came back the instant response.

"Because we think you being here is fascinating, and we want to spend some time with you," Lisa retorted. "Is there a reason why you stay here?" she added.

"Hurry" was the reply, followed by "stay" and "cellar."

"Are you staying in the cellar?" Lisa asked.

It replied, "Little altar."

The word *altar* refers, of course, to any structure upon which offerings or sacrifices are made as part of a religious ceremony. Altars are usually found at shrines and are located in temples, chapels, churches, and other centers of worship. Within City Hall the Minneapolis Police Department had a small chaplain's office located on the first floor; the chaplain would use this area to comfort those who had lost a loved one to crime. This room is currently abandoned due to economic cutbacks. It would also make sense that the infamous Chapel Courtroom (where Moshik and others were sentenced to death) was named due to the chapel that once resided there.

The phrase *little altar* would perhaps suggest a more makeshift and private focus for a religious practice, over a more permanent structure—this may have taken place under City Hall, amongst the dark, hidden labyrinth of tunnels and rooms (as the spirit suggested). Secrecy of worship is normally facilitated through fear of religious persecution or because the practice in question has a socially unacceptable ideology. There is also a possibility that Masonic ceremonies may have been performed; this organization draws its members heavily from the vocations of judges, politicians, attorneys, and men of the law—a secret meeting place for those members who worked throughout the building would not be an unreasonable suggestion.

Room 326 was the office of the Honorable Charles Burke Elliott, the judge who sentenced John Moshik to death. Judge Elliott is often referred to as the "Hanging Judge"—this is a term used to describe a judge who has gained a notorious reputation for applying the ultimate penalty, reflecting a strong moral desire for quick and firm justice. In opposition to this description, I discovered Judge Elliott's obituary, which referred to him as having "fairness and kindness—that matched his attainments in learning and activities for good."

He is described as a gentleman of great dignity with fine manners, kind and cordial, with a sense of humor and an air of serenity and calm. His tenure as a member of the Minnesota Supreme Court marked him as a jurist of unusual learning, great industry, sound judgment, and superior understanding of humanity. Perhaps people's passion for folklore has overtaken the forgotten facts regarding the judge's character.

Charles Burke Elliott was born on a farm in Morgan County, Ohio, on January 6, 1861. He moved to Minneapolis in 1884 after his studies to start his judicial career. His diaries for the years between 1884 and 1890 are an interesting record that reflects a grim determination to succeed despite numerous discouragements—he worked hard to become an established lawyer. In 1887 he earned his first academic distinction, granted by the University of Minnesota; this was the first degree for a Doctor of Philosophy ever conferred by the institution. In 1890 Governor William R. Merriam appointed Elliott to the municipal bench of Minneapolis—when Elliott was only twenty-nine years old. In 1894 he was advanced to a place on the district bench, where he remained until 1905, at which time he was appointed to the state supreme court by Governor John A. Johnson. Judge Elliott died on September 18, 1935. It was possible that he engaged with us by his office via the Ovilus; the unreasonable reflection upon his memory may have led him to stay *in situ* after his death—or his unwavering assiduity towards seeing fair justice administered.

After our exploration of City Hall I trawled through a myriad of historical paperwork connected to the judge. I was conscious of wanting to find a link to the words *little altar*—I was interested to see if I could uncover any religious background or unorthodox spiritual practices that the judge may have undertaken. I then found a transcription of the memorial speech given at Judge Elliot's funeral; it highlighted his beliefs: "He was unostentatiously a religious man, believing that religion is the basis of civil society." The speech goes on to state that he was a lifelong member of the Episcopal Church, having been confirmed at Trinity Church in Minneapolis in 1884, and was later an attendee of St. Mark's Church. Interestingly, it then mentions that he was a Knight Templar and a Shriner.

Strange Masonic Practices

A Shriner is a member of the Ancient Arabic Order of the Nobles of the Mystic Shrine, established in 1870, and like the Knights Templar is a branch of Freemasonry. Freemasonry requires its members to engage in secretive religious practices and believes in the ideology of a Supreme Being— although the term is subject to the conscience of the individual. Due to this belief, Freemasonry accepts men from various religious backgrounds; this then requires Freemasonry to use the term *Volume of the Sacred Law* as a generic name for any religious book. I have documented this because Freemasonry dictates the *Volume of the Sacred Law* to be present on an altar during their practices—it is kissed when prospective candidates bow before the altar. This indicates how intrinsic an altar is to the ceremonial procedures of Freema-

Minneapolis City Hall

sonry, and could support the claim that secret Masonic gatherings were taking place below ground.

During the Ovilus interaction a strange feeling overcame several members of the team; they claimed that someone was pulling them—not in a physical sense, but as a projected desire onto them—to get them to leave the location. Perhaps pulling them towards the cellar (although I would describe Minneapolis City Hall has having a basement rather than a cellar). The basement is now bright, open, and airy—with tables, chairs, and a few vending machines (originally it would have been dark and difficult to navigate with an end-less maze of uncharted areas). The sub-basement contains numerous maintenance offices for mechanics and clean-ers and has a heady infusion of paint and mechanics' grease hanging in the air.

There are public pedestrian tunnels connecting the build-ing to the Hennepin County Government Center under 5th Street and to the U.S. Courthouse under 4th Street. There are also restricted tunnels for use by the sheriff connecting under 4th Avenue to the Hennepin County jail and to the Government Center. Unfortunately, public access to the base-ment is limited, and the majority of the space has changed considerably since Judge Elliott's day; this means that any further investigation of the judge and the altar will remain a mystery.

The very concept of a secret, makeshift altar would lead me to believe that nothing would ever be found, even if per-mission were given to fully explore the basement and it was how it used to look. Everything cannot always be solved, and some questions will always remain unanswered—historians can never fully know because they were never there; paranor-mal investigators can never fully know because they aren't there. This makes me doubly frustrated.

CONCLUSION

I was disappointed that no contact was made with John Moshik, and it was frustrating that our trigger objects did not move—after hearing the tales of poltergeist activity in the building. The unraveling of Charles Elliott and his Masonic background was intriguing though and only discovered after the investigation; it would be interesting for me to go back in the future and try to engage further with Charles. I would want to ask him how he feels about having the moniker of "Hanging Judge" associated with his name.

Minneapolis City Hall stubbornly clings on to its historical importance—it was added to the National Register of Historic Places in 1974. Its formalism represents a unique moment in time, when other examples have been lost under the evolutionary hammer of modernity. The central clock tower is 345 feet high and was once the tallest structure in Minneapolis, until the Foshay Tower was constructed in the late 1920s. In the decades since its construction, City Hall went from being the tallest building in downtown Minneapolis to one of the shorter ones. Sightseers only serendipitously stumble upon City Hall now due to the gaps left between the Babelesque constructions of the latter twentieth century that swamp it under a skyscraper blanket of glass and metal. It is frustrating that we can longer see its impressive, unmistakable beauty outlined against the Minneapolis skyline as our ancestors may have done, but I guess we should be grateful that it is still there at all.

CHAPTER 2

The Palmer House Hotel

SAUK CENTRE

Native American spirits, the apparition of a small boy, haunting music, and a ghostly gray humanoid figure are all interwoven into the legend of the Palmer House Hotel.

The Palmer House Hotel in Sauk Centre, Stearns County, is one of the most paranormally active buildings you could ever wish to investigate. AAA's *Going Places* magazine listed the Palmer House Hotel in the top five of the most haunted hotels in America—it is also one of Stearns County's most historic and architecturally important buildings. I have investigated the Palmer House more than any other building in America, and I would not disagree with that assessment.

I first became aware of the Palmer House through local tales of ghostly happenings and the stories told by other paranormal investigators. I have benefited greatly from staying in the Palmer House for long periods of time, and I have conducted numerous investigations there—my paranormal experiences in this chapter are a condensing of these investigations. Subsequently I have held vigils, at some time or another, in every location within the hotel with every possible combination of my team. Of course there have been times when I would sit for hours in the hotel with little happening, but the rate at which paranormal contact is made appears greater than at most other locations. The depth and strength of my evidence is also in part due to the owner Kelley Freese and her willingness to accommodate my team while running a fully functioning hotel, restaurant, and bar. Kelley has also contributed to this chapter with her expertise and knowledge of local history.

HISTORY

The Sauk Centre Area Historical Society is situated in the basement of the town's library and provided me with a location to conduct my research. They have every copy of the *Sauk Centre Herald*, published weekly from 1868 to the present day (during a six-month period I managed to turn every page and look at every article). I also accessed maps, plans, photographs, period books, and obituaries.

The first building to be erected on the site of the Palmer House Hotel was the Sauk Centre House, built in 1863 by Alexander Moore. He also planned the entire layout of the town, and the positioning of the hotel would have been one of his main deliberations. W. F. Barnard did the surveying and Moore filed the first plat, which consisted of thirty-three blocks. Built prominently on the main crossroads of

The Sauk Centre House

the town, all of the other buildings would have been erected in relation to the Sauk Centre House. The population of the town and surrounding area barely reached a couple of hundred at this time, but the townsfolk wanted expansion and the business it would bring; a hotel and hostelry that could be used to host celebrations, meetings, and gatherings was required. What they gained was a cool-white wooden structure that gleamed out of the dust and heat of this frontier town. It had clean Greek Revival lines, a graceful veranda, a pediment roofline, returning eaves, and wide raking boards; this inspired Stearns County historian Bill Morgan to describe it in the *St. Cloud Times* as "a slice of New England grandeur set down on the Stearns County prairie"—an architectural gem in a then-dystopic world.

The Palmer House, Sauk Centre (Photo by Ron Jamiolkowski)

This quickly evolving yet embryonic town could already boast to having three stores, a sawmill, a flour mill, a cabinet shop, a cooperage, and a tannery. Despite this rapid expansion, however, Sauk Centre was still a untamed area, and the people who populated this growing hamlet had to be full of the pioneering spirit—this was illustrated through the reporting of wolf attacks on both people and cattle in 1866 and the regular sighting of bears just wandering through the streets.

NATIVE AMERICAN MYTHOLOGY AND SPIRITS

Some of the paranormal activity associated with the hotel could easily be steeped in Native American folklore; I firmly believe that an entity visits the basement that is *from the Earth* and not human (an elemental). Native American cultures are familiar with such entities, like the legendary Pukwudgie (a small troll with smooth, gray skin and a large nose and ears). This energy has made its arrival known to me via the heavy smell of sulfur and the act of engulfing investigators in blackness—so they completely disappear on a night vision camera (as if a dark blanket has been thrown over them); doglike snuffling and growling noises have also been recorded on my equipment. Although not evil in the biblical sense of the word, it is sometimes best not to engage or give the power of acknowledgment to some of the darker forces I encounter (that are just passing through). It is noticeable though that paranormal activity appears to cease around the time this entity makes itself known—perhaps the smaller fish swim away when the big fish arrives.

The first hotel was built barely a year after the Sioux Uprising—for which a stockade was erected in 1862 to protect the town (fear of more Indian reprisals must have been ever present in the minds of the townsfolk). The land it was constructed on was of strategic and religious importance to the Ojibwe and the Dakota Sioux long before Sauk Centre existed. Five very large burial mounds (one of which was 200 feet long) occupied most of the north bank directly after the river crossing, and traces of the earthworks can still be seen on the peninsula (despite their excavation at the beginning of the twentieth century). The 1825 Treaty of Prairie du Chien made the whole area a "no-man's land"—bloodshed was common if the two tribes stumbled across one another accidently on hunting expeditions along the Sauk River. Sauk Centre itself was named after five exiled Sauk Indians who made their homes on the banks of Sauk Lake—they were also killed after clashing with Dakota Sioux in the latter part of the eighteenth century.

In 1857 Alexander Moore led a team of workers in constructing a dam on the Sauk River; they witnessed an all-day battle that took place in the water between the Ojibwe and the Dakota Sioux that resulted in many casualties. The workers documented that the dead warriors were buried where they fell, and artifacts have been unearthed around the riverbank and surrounding land to support this claim. It would be reasonable to suggest that paranormal activity is strong on this land due to the energy of the Native American conflicts that took place there—as a consequence, negative entities could easily feed on that energy.

BRINGING NEGATIVITY FROM THE BATTLEFIELD

The location of the Sauk Centre House became strategically important for both the U.S. Army and politicians; General Winfield Hancock set up his new headquarters in St. Paul in the spring of 1869, and the Sauk Centre House became a regular stopping-off point for high-ranking senior officers traveling north to inspect the forts (erected quickly to suppress the Dakota Sioux uprisings). Prominent officers, including General Hancock, were accompanied by influential politicians like Alexander Ramsey, Sir William McDougall (a prominent Canadian diplomat), and Senator William Windom. General Hancock's first documented stay was reported in the *Sauk Centre Herald* on September 2, 1869:

> General Hancock and staff consisting of General Hartruff, General Baird, General Greene, and Colonel Walker, Colonel Gillman, Captain Wheaton and F. P. Lambert, stopped at Barnum's Hotel Tuesday evening

and left Wednesday morning on their way to the Forts above, whither General Hancock is going on a tour of inspection. Two of the Minnesota Stage Co.'s two fine Concord coaches were chartered for the trip.[5]

Perhaps the best known Army officer to stay at the hotel during this period was General Philip Henry Sheridan, who was famous for his role in defeating Robert E. Lee during the Civil War; his stay was reported on June 23, 1870:

Major General Phil. Sheridan, accompanied by his attaches passed through Sauk Centre on Wednesday morning on his way to the frontier. He has been taking a tour of inspection to the several frontier forts in the department of Dakota, coming across the country from the Missouri River.[6]

It is possible that the generals and military men (fresh from the battlefield) would have the negative energy of warfare attached to them—the pain and anguish of killing. This could easily seep into the fabric of the building during the times they stayed there and could further feed negative entities. Native American warriors were aware of this phenomenon; they would have performed clearing exercises at the end of a battle to rid themselves of the paranormal mire that attached itself to them. Certainly any Native Americans in spirit would have taken great offense to the generals. Due to previous encounters and engagements they would have had with the U.S. Army, I suspect they would have also been aware of their journey to further engage with tribal members at their final destination.

INVESTIGATION

The Smoky Apparition

In my opinion, the bar is the most active part of the hotel; there has been more contact in this area than in any other location. On one memorable vigil I was standing behind the bar in the dark, having turned off all the electrical appliances and lights; I asked if anyone could hear me and whether they could give me a sign of their presence. At that exact moment all of the lights behind the bar came back on. This made me laugh, due to the brilliance of the sign; I joked that they could now really impress me and fix me a drink (which they didn't do). I turned the lights off and started the vigil again, but this time the atmosphere changed. When my K2 EMF meter started to spike into the red, I knew something was imminent, but I was not prepared for what came next.

Suddenly I saw a full-bodied apparition appear before my eyes in a humanoid shape to my left-hand side—about six feet away from me. I turned so we faced one another, and I stood my ground, waiting to see what would happen next. It started to walk towards me in a fog of diaphanous, dirty, gray smoke. For a millisecond I tried to work out what I should do next—as it moved to within three feet of me; then it just dissipated, like somebody trying to disperse cigar smoke. Seconds later it reappeared, almost on top of me. It forced me to take a step backwards; it started to re-form into a humanoid shape again, growing and spreading low to my left, but this time it never quite made a full body and it disappeared again. It did not appear for a third time. There was no need to ask the team if they had also seen it—the look on their faces told me everything.

A ghostly, gray humanoid figure walks along
the corridor of the second floor from Room One

I later discovered that the hotelier Al Tingley (the joint owner of the hotel in the 1970s) had published a book in 1984 called *Corner on Main Street: True Story of the Innkeepers on Sinclair Lewis Avenue*, in which he describes the same entity in one of his chapters. He saw the same smoky, gray humanoid moving down the corridor towards him on the second floor, coming from what is now Room One. He claimed the apparition had been seen regularly from the 1950s and 1960s onwards, by guests and staff alike. I had not known this information when I saw the entity, and I was pleased and reassured that I had described the experience in exactly the same way Al had done. On a separate investigation, the Minnesota Ghosts team captured what appeared to be the same entity on video—from a static camera set up in the lobby facing the bar. I wanted to research and find out who or what this apparition was; I then discovered there would be no lack of candidates.

To add to the paranormal soup of accidents, incidents, illnesses, murders, and Native American bloodshed is the energy and activity that any historical hotel brings. What is encapsulated within the square red-brick walls of the Palmer House is a transient microcosm of humanity: people have been conceived there; people have been born there; people have been married there; people have worked, eaten, drunk, and slept there; and people have died there, so they subsequently haunt there. As the turnover of people historically coming through the building is extensive, any identification of the gray apparition would be difficult.

The sole reason the Sauk Centre House came into existence was due to its location in terms of passing trade; in 1859 the Minnesota Stage Company actually extended its lines through Sauk Centre, as they realized the town was perfectly positioned on the edge of fertile prairie. The town was destined to become the trading center for the ever-increasing numbers of people who came to make their homes in the Sauk Valley. They even erected a stage office in the hotel lobby. Passing business was also welcomed from the road between St. Cloud and Alexandria and through its prominence on the Red River trail—as highlighted by Sauk Centre historian Ivy Hildebrand:

> One of the early advantages to Sauk Centre was its location on an important Red River trail from Fort Garry (now Winnipeg, Canada), and Pembina, on the Red River just south of the Canadian boundary, to St. Paul. This Sauk Valley route had become increasingly popular after 1849, not only because it was shorter than the other routes, but also because it lay within Chippewa territory rather than the more dangerous Sioux lands along the Minnesota River. It was 448 miles from Pembina to St. Paul on the Sauk Valley Route, so any settlement along the way provided a welcome break in the long journey.[7]

The increase in population and visitors to Sauk Centre resulted in the deaths of more people; the hotel would now function as a makeshift infirmary to the townsfolk. Diphtheria (a contagious respiratory illness spread through direct contact or through the air, characterized by a sore throat, fever, and skin lesions) swept through the county, and many people would have died in the hotel as a result. One such unfortunate incident was that of William Casebeer, who died of "lung fever" on February 7, 1868, in one of the guest rooms. A brief report in the *Herald* on February 20, 1868, outlines how underprepared and ill-equipped a remote Midwestern town was during this era:

> At the Sauk Centre House on the 7th inst. of lung fever, William Casebeer formerly of Summerset County, Penn., aged about 20 years old. Mr. C was an honest, upright and industrious young man of good moral habits and was respected by all who knew him. He died away from home but among friends. Though the day was piercing cold, a large number attended the remains to the grave. The funeral service was read by Rev. A. K. Fox.[8]

The Ghost Boy

Spiritualism and mediumship have always been part of the hotel in all of its incarnations, a practice that is still upheld today. Recorded in the *Herald* on April 30, 1868, with an eye to promoting its guests, the Sauk Centre House posted the following:

> Prof. Sands, the world-renowned Magician and Ventriloquist and his lady, the unrivalled Astrologist and impressible medium, have arrived in Sauk Centre and are stopping at Barnum's hotel, where Mrs. S can be consulted with regard to the past present and future; and the Prof. will give two grand Entertainments at the school House on Friday and Monday Evenings, May, 1st and 4th. Prof. Sands' reputation as a performer is too well known to require any remarks from us.[9]

Professor H. Sands was a skilled performer and was listed on the bill of the Fairchild's Hall in Madison as far back as 1854. Unfortunately, tragedy struck his family during their stay at the Sauk Centre House; on May 7, 1868, the hotel stairs claimed their first victim:

> Accident—A Difficult Situation: Last week a little child of Prof. Sands', about 5 years old, fell off the stairs at Barnum's hotel, falling on the head and smashing in the skull on the back part of the head. Dr. Palmer was immediately sent for, who raised the skull off the brain—a most difficult operation.[10]

There was never a follow-up to this story to outline whether the boy recovered or not, but it is interesting to note that many psychics, employees, and guests have witnessed a small boy playing on the stairs and that these sightings were recorded long before I uncovered the evidence of an accident taking place.

The interest in Spiritualism was thriving throughout the Midwest during this period, and many lectures and séances took place in the Sauk Centre House (the town's citizenry provided a ready-made, willing audience); this is shown during the week of August 9, 1872, when five séances were practiced by J. L. Potter and H. H. Smith:

> Spiritualism—Messrs. J. L. Potter and H. H. Smith, who lectured here last fall, are coming again and will give four or five lectures, commencing August 9th.

The following year Mr. Potter was back, and he once again performed his skills in front of an enthusiastic Sauk Centre audience:

> December 6, 1873: Spiritualism—J. L. Potter, trance speaker, who travels under the auspices of a State Society or organization of Spiritualists lectured here five evenings ending on Sunday last. Our Citizens manifested their usual liberality and willingness to hear new theories and doctrines by a large attendance.

A History of Hauntings

Edward Barnum owned and managed the hotel from 1867 until 1870 and employed many staff—including bellhops, clerks, cooks, maids, and bar workers. One of those employees was an odd-job man named Moses; he is mentioned in a story printed on April 14, 1870, which provides us with a unique historical insight into how hauntings (even back then) were intrinsic to the hotel's fabric. It would suggest that even during this period ghosts were present in the forefront of the minds of the staff who worked there:

> Moses, the American citizen of African descent who makes himself useful around Barnum's hotel, threw a stone at a gentleman one night last week, who had a basket over his head personating a ghost. The stone went through the basket just above his head. Playing ghost may be jolly fun, but a little dangerous.[11]

Several months after this event Moses died—I'm sure the shock he received that night had a detrimental effect on his heart condition:

> Moses, the Negro man who was employed around Barnum's hotel, and who had been sick for several months, died on Friday night of last week. He had been able to be about for several days previous to his death, but was in a very weak condition, and his mind in a demented state. On Friday he became crazed and raved around, when Deputy Sheriff Dennis took him in charge intending to start to St. Cloud with him on Saturday morning to procure an order to have him taken to the insane asylum, but he was relieved from his troubles before morning by the hand of death. A *post mortem* examination was held over his body, which showed his heart to be almost entirely to be decayed.[12]

I have included this information because it suggests the hotel was haunted, even back then—the prank would not have been in the mind of the perpetrator otherwise and the reaction to it not as strong. We know the Sauk Centre House was built in 1863, and this incident took place in 1870; that leaves only the Native American spirits, the military visits, the Spiritualism, William Casebeer, and the possible death of the boy as considerations for the paranormal activity they experienced back then.

The Residual Music

Many of the investigations I have undertaken at the Palmer House Hotel have provided me with the same common paranormal phenomena. Throughout the vigils I can hear the sound of polka music bleeding through the white noise and intermittent radio broadcasts of my ghost box.

Two factors lead me to believe that this music is paranormal in nature: first, I set the ghost box to receive only the AM signal—as this provides a larger selection of talk radio broadcasts (there are noticeably fewer music stations on this waveband). Second, it is not common to hear dated polka music played on any radio station—especially at the times of the night I investigate. With this in mind I started to look for period documentation, to see if there had been a history of this music being played in the hotel, to try and uncover why this haunting residual sound was coming through with such regularity.

It became clear that the town's celebrations during the nineteenth century were centered on the Sauk Centre House; one of its earliest functions provided me with the first documented article written on the hotel, from the *St. Cloud Democrat* in 1866, when fifty couples gathered for a wedding ceremony on New Year's Eve. It was hosted by Peter Safford, a longtime resident of Sauk Centre:

> Mine host, Safford, gave a party which was the largest ever given at that place.[13]

It must have been quite an event, celebrating both the new year and a marriage in this fledgling hotel, complete with good food and music—I daresay remembered fondly by the townsfolk who were in attendance.

Warren Adley ran the hotel in 1867 and allowed the building to host the town's Fourth of July celebrations that year. A temporary wooden raised platform was erected next to the hotel on its east side for dancing, with a carnival and firework display also organized. According to the *Sauk Centre Herald*, the partying continued at the hotel long into the night, with dancing, music, and food; the article also states, "There was no drunkenness, and everyone was well behaved."

I researched further to try and uncover a regular organized dance with clockwork regularity that could leave a residual haunting, rather than the random or annual celebrations that were taking place. The next owner of the hotel was Edward Barnum, who was described as a great entertainer and host; he instigated the Russell's Calico Dance on May 6, 1868. This was described as one of the most interesting occasions in the town's history. It was reported that the costumes were made of everything from silk to horse blankets and showed the extent to which "the joyous-minded citizens would go in order to have a good time." Admission was fifty cents, which paid for supper and a full evening of dancing; a local fiddler named Taylor was accompanied by his wife in the playing of waltzes, polkas, and square dances.

It soon became evident in my research that the hotel was at the center of an excess of dancing and gaiety during this period. This assiduity for making merry was actually reported on acerbically by the editor of the *Sauk Centre Herald* during the winter of 1874, when he retorted that "three dances in town during the last week was putting them in pretty thick!"

He also passed comment in September 1869 on the absurdity of the latest dance craze to be seen at the Sauk Centre House:

> The latest female abomination is the "kangaroo skip." They lap the hands, keep their arms close to the sides, and go skipping and jumping, hopping and bouncing, very much like the kangaroo. This in connection with the camel's hump and the diminutive boot heels, makes their motions as graceful as the strut of a lame Shanghai in the wet grass, reminds one of the ruralist's opinion of the jig dancer, who looked like he was trying to shake a shilling down his trouser leg.[14]

Clearly, some tuition was required in the art of dancing if one was to attract the attentions of the opposite sex. On February 6, 1868, Barnum posted an ad in the *Herald* outlining the virtues of good instruction in this area; this provided me with the organized regularity I was hoping to find:

> The dancing school and cotillion, parties organized some five weeks ago under the management of Mr. M. R. Seaman, still goes on. Every Saturday evening about 20 couples of "fair women and brave men" congregate at Barnum's hotel to join in the social dance and keep time to "music by the band." Prof. Seaman as a "dancist" gives entire satisfaction; Taylor's band furnishes the best of music, while the school, as a school, is a success.[15]

Barnum certainly began to see the economic benefits of hosting regular dances at the hotel. This was despite some of the more negative comments made in town at the way in which young ladies conducted themselves on the dance floor. Barnum even promoted these social gatherings with no admission fee—as this example from 1867 illustrates:

> Attention dancists—Mr. Fred H. Russell requests us to announce to all lovers of the social dance that on Friday evening, March 7th, (one week from tomorrow) he will give a free dance at Barnum's hotel. It is Mr. Russell's intention to get up a series of cotillion parties, and for this purpose will give a free dance on the first evening, at which time parties wishing to join for the series can have an opportunity. Mr. Russell is a good violinist, a first class caller, is some on the dance, and is in every way competent. A general invitation is extended to all.[16]

This trend continued, and Barnum even began to throw in a free supper:

> March 5, 1868—Tomorrow evening a free dance comes off at Barnum's Hotel, to be given by Mr. Fred H. Russell. Mr. Barnum will, on the occasion, give a free supper. Free dance, free music, and free lunch— what more could you ask? A large attendance is anticipated.[17]

I decided to instigate an experiment due to the evidence I had uncovered of regular organized dancing taking place at the hotel. In the lobby next to the piano is a remarkable handle-driven antique gramophone player, complete with two racks of fragile records (hiding a treasure trove of long-forgotten polkas and waltzes). I placed a random record onto the turntable and rotated the crank handle a considerable number of times; as the record revolved, the handsomely crafted silver needle arm smoothly dropped into the waiting groove. Hissing and popping became audible, followed by the opening rich, deep musical notes of a bygone era, breaking beautifully through the crackling.

The music flooded the lobby and transported the area into an age of dancing and best dresses. As the first few notes filled the air, it was noticeable that the atmosphere in the whole hotel had changed; it was like a historical call to every spirit, reminding them of memories from when they were alive—beckoning them to come and congregate with us. As I stood by the stairs I was nearly knocked over by a cascade of rushing wind that went through me on its way into the lobby—as entities rushed from all parts of the hotel to engage with the music and nostalgic fun. The EMF meter in my hand spiked furiously into the red and stayed there for some considerable time—registering a reading of over 20 milligauss.

Outlaws

During the 1880s the hotel allegedly turned into a Wild West–type gambling house and possible brothel. (This information was passed onto me through third parties by other teams and psychics and cannot be verified.) Several of the spirits and ghosts are thought to be from this era—when life was cheap, and many women were abused or believed to be murdered.

I have found no proof that the hotel was run as a brothel (and I have searched extensively); this would be in reference to the old Sauk Centre House, which was a completely different building from the Palmer House—with different room layouts. The Sauk Centre House was only a two-story building, unlike the current three-story Palmer House, so any incidents that were a catalyst for a haunting on the top floor (Room Seventeen, for example) would have needed to have taken place above the roof of the old two-story building.

I read every page of every published *Sauk Centre Herald* and never once found an article concerning a murder in the town connected to the hotel. In a small community, where the weekly news consists of documenting how many fish were caught in the local lake, a murder would have made a very prominent headline. I also failed to find any articles describing serious lawlessness in the hotel, even though other, less prominent hotels (away from Main Street) would regularly be mentioned for incidents of fighting and the theft of personal belongings and horses.

It is also worth noting that the most prominent building in town, situated at the main crossroads, would not be a good location for a gentleman wanting to embrace this kind of activity without being noticed in a small community where everyone knows everyone else. The townsfolk did celebrate though when the Sauk Centre House finally burned down in 1900, but that had more to do with modernity; the old pioneer wooden architecture was seen to be an eyesore when every other building on Main Street was now a modern brick-built construction. The town saw this as an opportunity to build a state-of-the-art hotel fit for the new twentieth century, and that is what they got.

Christena and Ralph Palmer with their daughter, circa 1898

The new hotel was built by Ralph Palmer and used the same substructure and basement foundations as the old hotel—but that is where the similarities end. It opened in 1901 and became the first building in Sauk Centre to have electricity—subsequently, the switches had to be replaced after six months due to guests continually turning the lights on and off (in a moment of awe and wonder). The Art Nouveau–styled interior that we see today—with its Viennese stained-glass windows, tin ceilings, and ornate carved butternut staircase—was a million miles from the old Sauk Centre House.

There is evidence to suggest that outlaws did stay in the building; Cole Younger of the Young/James gang enjoyed the hospitality of the hotel—as he toured the state with a lecture series in 1903. The negative spirits of a gambling house and brothel could have been brought into the building this way.

The Basement

The wife of Ralph Palmer was Christena Palmer; she died in 1936 but still resides in the hotel. We have become very good acquaintances through the many conversations I've had with her—she comes through very strongly and quickly on the ghost box when I ask to speak to her (within minutes normally). During one conversation I asked her to spell her name—I had seen both "Christena" and "Christina" used in historical texts; much to my amazement and that of my team, she clearly stated, "With an 'e'."

I said, "Thank you. From now on I will spell your name with an 'e'." So it is now Christena Palmer with an "e."

The basement is a location that has a lot of repression and heavy sadness about it. It was through my research that I may have discovered the reason why; during the early part of the last century, flu epidemics swept through Stearns County, and many Sauk Centre residents lost their lives. The freezing Minnesota winters render the earth solid, and burials could only be instigated by warming the ground days before the funeral by lighting a fire. This would have been a difficult task to maintain during an epidemic, with people dying more quickly than they could be buried.

I believed that the Palmer House basement may have been used as a makeshift morgue, until such time the backlog could be cleared. There would have been few areas available in Sauk Centre for this kind of storage, and it was cool enough and sufficiently hidden from the public's gaze. The depression of grieving, coupled with the sad, negative thoughts of entities contemplating a life cut short, may be washing over the basement during our vigils.

Room One

I was booked into Room One on my first visit to the Palmer House. It is located on the second floor and is the farthest room to your right as you climb the stairs. As I placed my travel bag on the bed to unpack, I suddenly became startled by the loud sound of a woman sobbing uncontrollably. I dropped everything and rushed next door into the bathroom to see who this was (there was nobody there). Activity like this leaves you questioning your own sanity as you try to logically figure out what happened to you. The crying was very loud and sounded real; it had forced me to sprint next door, where I was expecting to comfort a distressed woman.

Room One is located on the southeast corner and thus has two outside walls; the third wall is next to the corridor that I checked and was empty, and the fourth wall is the dividing wall to Room Two, which was unoccupied. It was impossible to believe that this loud, distinctive sound could have come from anywhere else but my room; if all other normal explanations have been ruled out, then by default it becomes paranormal activity (experiences that fall outside of the normal range of experience or scientific explanation).

CONCLUSION

Some entities with which I would have expected to have made contact during my extensive investigations have eluded me—such as the boy on the stairs, seen by everyone else but me, it seems. I have no reason to disbelieve the accounts of the staff and various guests, especially after I found the evidence of a trauma and possible death after the sightings were documented.

I also wanted to contact Sinclair Lewis during my time there; he was the first American to win the Nobel Prize for Literature and was employed in the hotel in 1902, as a bellhop and night clerk. He was very clumsy and broke many things—much to the consternation of Ralph Palmer—including the glass in the cigar display cabinet in the lobby (as described in his journal).

Lewis became more engrossed with his writing, which caused him to forget to call a guest with a requested early-morning wakeup call. The guest subsequently missed his

train; this was the final straw, and Lewis was fired. He then
wrote about the hotel in his seminal 1920 novel *Main Street*,
calling it the *Minniemashie Hotel*; it is believed he still roams
around the building, but I have never seen him. Only once
in the basement did I get the name "Red" coming through on
the ghost box—but it never engaged with me further. (Sinclair Lewis was called "Red" throughout his life.)

The interactions I've had with Christena and the witnessing of the gray humanoid figure, combined with the crying
in Room One and the haunting music, would suggest that
the Palmer House is paranormally active (it is unusual to
have such strong, differing events all happening in the same
location). The ghostly characters differ due to the historical
nature of the hotel and the land it is built on; they encompass a wide spectrum of individuals including outlaws, movie
stars, authors, businesspeople, tourists, and fallen Indian
warriors. Many of the entities I have encountered still think
they are working at the hotel: the barmen, bellhops, receptionists, hostlers, kitchen staff, chambermaids, dish washers,
and craftsmen are sometimes unhappy that the Englishman
(with his questions and equipment) is getting in the way of
their jobs—especially when there are beds to be made, sheets
to be washed, drinks to be served, and stables to be swept.

What I ultimately discovered is that the Palmer House is
not just any haunted hotel in a small, sleepy town in the middle of the Midwestern plains (now bypassed by the transient
traffic of Interstate 94). It is a jewel in the crown of American
social history, where paranormal investigators now make reservations in the hope of getting a bad night's sleep.

CHAPTER 3

The Mounds Theatre

St. Paul

Spirits from desecrated burial mounds, an apparition in a suit, and the ghost of a grumpy projectionist, await those planning a trip to this theater.

The Mounds Theatre is probably the site I have visited the most after the Palmer House; it was the first building I investigated in America, and a location I have accessed many times over the last four years. The majority of the evidence described in this chapter was from an initial week-long investigation (this was ideal as it allowed me to leave the equipment out untouched so I was able to record vast amounts of data without fear of contamination) and then subsequent follow-ups. It would be reasonable to say that whenever I visit the Mounds Theatre I come away with what could be described as a paranormal experience or encounter.

The historical research for the theater was different from the Palmer House, as very little was documented in local period newspapers—other than to say what was playing that week. The Minnesota Historical Society in St. Paul has a folder on the theater that presented me with planning regulation documents and bills for repair work and extensions to the property; these papers contained the names of the proprietors and gave me enough information to follow other leads—including key obituaries. I also interviewed many local people—this gave me valuable primary source material. I also discovered several film trade publications from the 1930s that contained detailed descriptions of the theater's interior during its refurbishment. The owner also had a good collection of documents and photographs that allowed me to expand my research further.

HISTORY

The Mounds Theatre is situated on Hudson Road on St. Paul's east side. It was opened in 1922 as a venue for silent movies and live entertainment. It was designed by architect C. A. Buetow and cost $22,000 to build; the layout incorporated a lobby, balcony, and 8,600 square feet of floor space. Under the ownership of John A. Freiermuth, the theater quickly became the hub of the neighborhood, playing to packed auditoriums of over 700 people. During the Great Depression people looked to the newly built theater as a form of escapism from the harsh realities of everyday living; they sat on the edge of their seats in suspense, rolled in the aisles with laughter, and cried a romantic tear—their emotions accompanied by the live orchestra. Its role within the community strength-

The Mounds Theatre, circa 1950

ened further when it was used during the day as a temporary food station—providing much-needed sustenance to those who were on the sharp end of the economy. It became a focal point for a town down at the heel: a place to meet, chat, and share stories.

THE ENERGY

I think it should be noted that the building has a reverential energy; it is the residual energy of getting up and performing, that electrical buzz of 700 patrons all experiencing the same feeling at the same time as one. It is the smell of the electricity, the feel of the plush red cinema seats, the thrill of a stolen kiss in the darkness, the anticipation, an actor applying makeup, an orchestra tuning their instruments, the spell of Hollywood, and the sound of distant, metronomic, soothing clicking as old celluloid film travels through the spools of a flickering projector. That energy and the reverential space of an auditorium can only be found in one other place outside of a theater—in a church.

That sense of this grandeur and romanticism can be historically attributed to Moses Finkelstein and Isaac Ruben, who bought the property in 1925; they renovated the theater extensively in the style of the avant-garde. Finkelstein and Ruben owned the majority of Minnesota's theaters and cinemas during the 1920s—their portfolio boasted over 120 theaters across the Midwest. Finkelstein was a jeweler from Lithuania who settled in St. Paul in 1880; Ruben was born in New York and owned a diminutive theater in Des Moines. With Finkelstein's land and Ruben's knowledge, they opened their first movie theater together in 1910—it was called the Princess and was located in St. Paul.

The duo expanded their business rapidly and built resplendent picture palaces throughout St. Paul and Minneapolis. Their powerful regional network allowed them to compete with the major U.S. cities for distribution rights to the latest and biggest films. Under the management of Bert Nix, the Mounds Theatre reopened in April 1925 with the silent film *North of 36*—one of the first Western adaptations from the novel by Emerson Hough. *Movieland Magazine* documented the grand event:

> St. Paul's Finest Suburban Theater: Redecorated and refurbished throughout, ablaze with a myriad of electric lights and signs that turned the corner of Hastings and Earl Streets into a rival of New York's Great White Way, Finkelstein and Ruben's new Mounds Theatre formally opened to the public, Saturday, April 11th.
>
> With its new decorative features, electrical effects, and new furnishings, the Mounds Theatre stands out

as one of the most beautiful suburban theaters in the Northwest. The new playhouse both inside and out is of beautiful design, in old rose and delft blue. The borders and designs are richly painted in black, gold, and orange. The ceiling divided into eight panels, is elaborately painted in gray, which has a stipple effect and black gold and orange designing. The beauty of these decorations has been enhanced by the skillful lighting and arrangement.

The lobby with its marble floor is attractively decorated in delft blue with a gold stipple effect. The woodwork has been done in old ivory and old rose trimming. The lobby is brilliantly lighted and opens into a foyer from which two staircases lead to the balcony, where patrons get a splendid view of the beautiful auditorium. Rich colored draperies which blend harmoniously with the decorations hang around the foyer and aisle entrances and are not a small feature in the beauty of the ensemble.[18]

The theater was renovated again in 1933 in the Art Deco style; the remodeling was partly due to the introduction of the "talkie" and the need to introduce a state-of-the-art sound system, to compete with the modernity of Hollywood. The Jazz Singer was released in 1927, and a slow redevelopment of the country's cinemas was taking place. When the Mounds Theatre reopened in 1933, the public was treated to the box-office smashes of the year, including 42nd Street, She Done Him Wrong, Little Women, and Morning Glory. This was now the golden era, when Clark Gable, Jean Harlow, Mae West, and Cary Grant played to amorous couples on a Friday night, only to make way for Roy Rogers and Buster Crabbe on a Saturday morning. This is when the auditorium would be filled with noisy children booing and cheering the villains and heroes under a hail of popcorn and jujubes. Each child who entered the theater in this era had a number printed on his or her ticket, and one lucky patron would find themselves going home for lunch with a new bicycle or a bat and ball courtesy of a lucky draw.

Developments came and went, as did patrons off to war, some never to grace the theater again. An early air conditioning system was introduced at the back of the stage that had its condensing coils cooled by the well water beneath the theater. Advances in electrical engineering saw the demise of the open electric-arc lamps in the projectors and an end to tedious trips to the basement for coal. This also made redundant the airtight, fireproof projection booths with their four-inch-thick metal doors. More refurbishments were carried out in the 1950s, and the films *Ben-Hur*, *On the Waterfront*, and *From Here to Eternity* kept the public moving through.

A STATE OF DISREPAIR

Unfortunately, it was not long before the Mounds Theatre's best years were behind it and the structure slowly fell into disrepair; cinema audiences fell in the 1960s and with them the capital to maintain the building. Television grew in popularity, and teenagers started to find themselves with a disposable income, allowing them to embrace pop culture financially—with its fashions, magazines, records, and live music; cinema seemed like the entertainment of their parent's generation. So in July 1967, after forty-five years of constant service and entertainment, the Mounds Theatre closed its doors to the public—thus hiding the shame of peeling paintwork, worn carpets, and gum-strewn seats.

Throughout the 1970s and 1980s, the theater became just a shell, nothing more than a hollow reminder to past glories, its leaky roof soiling the rundown computer hardware it stored in its makeshift role as a warehouse. That was the way it stayed until the old theater doors were pried open once more in 2001 by Jackie Day, who saw the potential of the building, as the first beams of light danced around the dilapidated dusty interior to illuminate the dream. Right there and then Jackie asked the owner, George Hardenbergh, if he would give her the property, and he promptly replied, "Yes!"

The theater was donated to Jackie's charity by Mr. Hardenbergh to address the unmet needs of the families of St. Paul's east side. Charity director Jackie led the renovation project, and with the help of a grant through the city of St. Paul and an anonymous donation, the Mounds Theatre once again became the landmark it is today. It opened for a second time in April 2003, only for Jackie to realize that it was not just the building she now possessed, but all the ghosts and spirits as well; the Mounds Theatre is now rightly recognized as one of the most paranormally active buildings in St. Paul.

INVESTIGATION

Shadow Figures in the Lobby

We begin our ghost tour like all good visits to the theater, by standing in the lobby. Dark shadow people are seen walking through this area; they have no features, and details are hard to see on their blurry forms. The old main entrance is now where the concessions are sold; residual energy from past patrons entering and exiting the movie theater over the last ninety years would be strong in this area. Jackie spoke of an incident when she was working late in the lobby, producing a poster. She started to walk towards the exit doors when she was grabbed by the shoulder and physically stopped from leaving. This was obviously very upsetting, and she now reasonably refuses to stay late on her own at night.

It is worth remembering that for 95 percent of the time the auditorium is empty; it is only frequented during rehearsals or for a couple of hours when a play or film is being shown. If an entity wanted to be undisturbed or wished to be in a quiet environment, this would be the ideal location—a luxury not afforded in a modern residential property. It could also be argued that if a ghost had the aspiration to be on the stage or a Hollywood star when they were living, then the theater could be used as a playground for those individuals to fulfill those dreams in the afterlife. If Jackie was quietly working all alone in the building, an assumption may have been made that the theater was empty and she may have caught an entity by surprise.

The Ghost in the Suit

One of our more experienced investigators, Warren, saw a full-bodied apparition appear in this area as he was collecting data. He was walking from the lobby to the dressing room when he happened to glance up and see a middle-aged man watching him through the open doors of the ticket booth area. The ghost followed him with his eyes and they exchanged looks—Warren described his demeanor as someone wanting to say, "Who are you?" and "What are you doing here?" The man was wearing clothes from the 1950s—with a period-styled brown tweed suit, yellow tie, and black swept-back hair. The intriguing part of this contact was the way in which Warren coherently described the entity as looking faded in color, like an old photograph, with the appearance of being completely flat and two-dimensional—like a cardboard cutout.

Warren's initial distress at being surprised by the entity, followed by his lucid, detailed description of the encounter, leaves me in no doubt this was a genuine experience. Then, as if he was never there, the ghost was gone—he showed himself just enough to be acknowledged and to make Warren aware that he was being watched. The bizarre nature of his flat, faded appearance could suggest that entities may arrive from other dimensions, where the rules of physics differ and distort the way we see their form. It is worth noting that a faded, flat humanoid moving around in the dark could easily be interpreted as a shadow figure. It could also be suggested that the energy of a ghost can dissipate over a period of time, like a battery becoming flat—this may then have an adverse affect on the brilliance of the manifestation. This loss of energy over a prolonged period of time may give an indication to why we rarely see apparitions outside of a 150-year window of history. If this were not the case we would still see manifestations of Neanderthal men wandering around from 600,000 years ago.

The Ghost of the Projectionist

Jackie took Lisa, Warren, and me upstairs to the projection booth; this is the most active area in the building, and the old projectionist resides here. He is a very unpleasant character according to those who have experienced contact with him; the whole atmosphere of the projection room is overwhelmingly heavy. It is a long, narrow corridor of a room with two old antique projectors facing out into the auditorium. They look big and cumbersome and fill the majority of the room with cold, gunmetal gray technology of a bygone age. The projectionist is offensive towards women and can be aggressive and physical; female members of staff have experienced swearing and objects thrown at them. He has appeared on several occasions and is described as a middle-aged man in smart dress of average height. Jackie and several staff have seen him appear in the corner of the projection booth, huddled over and crying. Our first contact with this projectionist would be on the stage.

To have the run of a haunted 1920s Art Deco theater to investigate was fantastic; a production of an Agatha Christie play was showing that week, and the set was of a 1930s English drawing room—with afternoon tea, cucumber sandwiches, a chaise lounge, a sofa, and all the accoutrements you would expect of a middle-class country house in an Agatha Christie murder mystery. I could feel the energy as I stepped onto the stage and looked out at the expanse of empty seats—which I could just make out in the gloomy darkness. I decided to sit on the stage as the rest of the team spread out around the auditorium; I felt very vulnerable as I sat there all alone in the darkness, with the lights and bleeps of the equipment chirruping around me. I had my back to the stage entrance and harbored the concern that an entity could come from the wings without my knowledge.

I decided to turn on the ghost box. I had barely switched on the device when it shouted the word *Red* in my headphones—I repeated what it said for the benefit of the team: "It came through very loud and said the word *Red* for some reason."

Somewhere out in the darkness I heard a gasp as Jackie took a sharp intake of breath.

"That's him! He's here. That's the name of the projectionist!" she said and practically fell over. Jackie had never told us the projectionist was named Red; this was a great start to the vigil, and it felt like he was just waiting for the box to be turned on so he could contact us.

I proceeded to have a disappointingly disjointed dialogue with Red before a new name came through—the name of Jim Dolan. I made a note of the information I was receiving, but it was not as fluent or as forthcoming as I would have hoped, especially after such a strong start.

The Interview

During the course of my investigations at the Mounds Theatre, the most incredible thing occurred. Jackie had managed to track down two elderly local men who had agreed to be interviewed about the theater and what it had been like in the 1940s and 1950s. I met with John and Ed and sat them down in the auditorium to be interviewed; I started asking them about their first experiences of going to the theater as small children to see black-and-white movies and "Saturday morning pictures." They suddenly sprang to life and became more animated as they discussed how much the admission was, what it was like inside, and even where the best girls used to sit. During the interview I asked, "Have you ever heard of a character named Red?"

"Sure," they said in unison—they were confirming information I had received through the ghost box.

"He used to work here. He died about ten years ago—he was a bit crazy but seemed like a friendly guy. He was once horsing around on the balcony and fell over the rail into the stalls below and broke his leg." Both men laughed as they recalled the incident.

"Can you remember Red's last name?" I inquired.

"It was something like Hoffman or Hoffmeyer."

I then asked, "Do you know a Jim Dolan?"

"Yes, Jimmy Dolan. He was an usher who died a few years ago. He was working one night and saw his girl in the back row with another man. He never got over it."

I corroborated the evidence I had previously received via the equipment with firsthand source material; no team member was aware of the information before we started the investigation. This justifies fully the faith I have in the equipment we use and our psychics. The two old guys continued to reminisce about stolen kisses, the size of popcorn portions, and the prizes they had won at the theater. I could not have been happier.

I took the information I received about Red and decided to use it in conjunction with the Ovilus. I went back to the stage and turned on the equipment; I asked if Red was there and explained what I was doing. The Ovilus then started repeating the same three words over and over again, relentlessly, for fifteen minutes:

"Fall—ouch—pain."

I broke the mantra by asking if he remembered falling off the balcony. After a short pause, the Ovilus replied:

"Remember."

The Haunted Projection Booth

During the baseline tests, a week previous to the investigation, I left a DVR running in the projection booth as I went through the rest of the building. When I played back the recording I could hear myself shut the heavy projection-booth door behind me—and seconds later I heard what sounded like a party starting. For the full thirty minutes the DVR was left running I could hear people talking in the background (nothing discernible, but definitely the sound of chatter). I could hear loud bangs like a door shutting, and there were two occasions when I could hear loud sniffs—like someone had come up close to the DVR to investigate; this became more significant later, when I was told that Red had been seen sobbing in this area.

We then tried to make further progress with Red. I turned on the ghost box and asked a series of questions; I asked if Red could tell me his last name—very quietly, almost as a meta-narrative running under the static, I heard and recorded the name "Hoffmeyer." I then asked who he thought the president was, and his reply came back instantly as "Eisenhower." This would place our spirit in a time frame between 1953 and 1961; it did not take long before Lisa also made contact psychically.

"He is standing next to me at the moment," she said.

"Can you see what he looks like?" I inquired.

"He's just a silhouette. I can only see a dark shadow." She raised her hand to show me how tall he was. "He is not happy. He is fed up with people who keep disturbing him."

"Do you have a message to give us? We can look for somebody if you want," I asked.

"I want you to contact Sarah," he said via Lisa.

"What is her last name?"

"Jorgen."

"Is that with a 'G' or a 'J'?"

"J"

"How old is she?"

"Eighty-seven."

"Where does she live?"

"St. Paul."

"Is there a message for her? What would you like us to say?"

"Tell her Eddie sent you." (It is possible that Red's first name was Edward.)

Then he said, "I will come after you [directed at me]. If you don't find her, I will get you!"

"I can only do my best. I will research and look, but I can't promise anything," I responded.

Lisa mirrored his reaction with a dismissive gesture of her hand, reflecting what she was seeing Red do. Then he left and went through the wall behind her. Extensive searches for Sarah have so far proved unsuccessful.

The Ghost on the Stage

On the stage another entity is known; a small girl has been seen in a pink dress—she is around five years old with a swatch of bright, blonde, curly hair. She is normally seen bouncing a ball around the stage and is sometimes only heard—as the sound of her ball slapping against the hollow wooden stage floor reverberates around the auditorium; this has been heard as far away as the lobby by staff and patrons alike.

The theater employees tell a tale of child disappearances taking place in the 1950s; to date these stories are without proof and could be nothing more than urban legend. I discussed this with a retired St. Paul police officer, and he did not recall any such incidents taking place. There was the macabre discovery of children's clothing by Jackie and her team during the renovation process that gave them cause for concern. A small child's shoe was found buried deep within the basement in the coal cellar, which by its design and style would indicate the period in question. A demolition of the projection-room office also revealed a small child's crumpled dress from the same era, hidden behind the pipe work (that could easily have belonged to the ghostly girl on the stage). It does seem odd that items of dated children's clothing should be discovered throughout the darkest recesses of the theater; your imagination would not have to work overtime to start putting some very dark thoughts together.

Just behind the stage to the left is an anteroom; this is a room where the electrical equipment is housed for the stage lights. I did some sweeps with a DVR in this area and gathered some interesting evidence. In between the team members

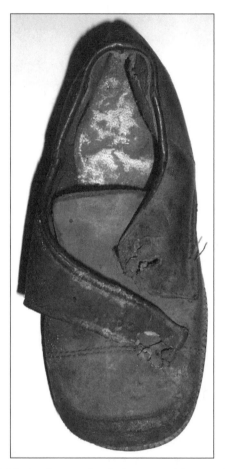

The child's shoe discovered in the basement of the Mounds Theatre

talking, you can clearly hear the recording of a small female child giggling. This was especially significant when you consider that the stage has the spirit of the girl playing on it. The second EVP was a man's voice that said, "It's a man!"

This can be placed into context, as the first team member who walked into the room and introduced himself to the spirits was Warren. Our recording could have picked up the conversation one spirit might be having with another to signal the arrival of our team member. Rather more bizarre was the next EVP we recovered: in the gaps left for a response, we clearly heard a man's voice say, "Three minutes."

We debated why a spirit would say, "Three minutes" in conjunction with the questions we were asking. The voice was clearly not one of the team, and we surmised that it may have been a stagehand informing an actor of when he is due on stage—a residual echo from the past.

I decided to focus on the small girl spirit for the next vigil and placed a large, shiny pink ball on the wooden stage boards as a trigger object—I arranged our equipment around it. I positioned a thermal imaging camera on the ball, in the hope that paranormal contact with the trigger object would result in a decrease in temperature, which I could measure. Several female members of the team started the vigil, as it was believed that a girl would be more likely to respond to a maternal figure when confronted by group of strangers. The team emphasized that the ball was there for the girl to play with.

During this process we noticed that the display of colors on the laptop linked to the thermal-imaging camera had changed—from yellow and orange to a cooler series of greens and blues; the temperature of the ball had actually dropped by 10 degrees Fahrenheit in under a minute. The ball quickly came back up to the ambient temperature of the stage again, without any noticeable outside influences. This significant temperature change, during such a short period of time, does not provide evidence on its own of a spirit girl interacting with the ball, but it does provide an unusual anomaly that would be difficult to explain.

A Violent Assault in the Basement

The basement is a dark, claustrophobic, and foreboding concrete hole that has no redeeming features; this is where a single, distressed, discarded shoe was found in amongst the rubbish. Jackie recalled a time when a member of the staff, upon hearing the sound of a girl playing, started the first line of the song, "If you're happy and you know it, clap your hands."

At which point a loud clap was heard; needless to say, she left the basement with some alacrity.

It is possible that the haunting incidents in this location were triggered by the desecration of Native American burial mounds close to the theater. The Mounds Theatre is so called due to the burial grounds that were destroyed in order to develop the Mounds Park area—as many as thirty-seven burial mounds were constructed in this area by the Hopewell culture 2,000 years ago (later, the Dakota Indians also used the same site to bury their dead). Upon their excavation, the remains of dead bodies were discovered along the bluffs— buried with artifacts indicating a religious process.

The mounds were initially excavated in 1856 by Edward Duffield Neill; this started a cycle of desecration that continued in 1869 with the construction of the railroad. In 1885 the rail yard was widened between the Mississippi and the remaining burial mounds by seventy-five feet, removing more of the site. In 1892 the city of St. Paul procured another seventeen acres, which included the remaining

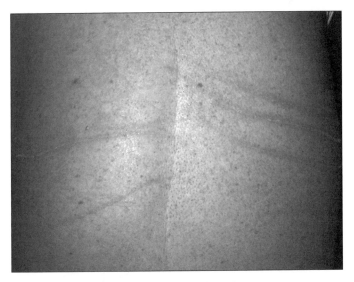

*The scratch marks from the assault on the investigator
in the Mounds Theatre basement*

mounds. They were re-landscaped four years later, destroying another eleven mounds in the process. In 1900 the park was expanded one last time to eighty-two acres, allowing for only a handful of the mounds to remain.

I started the vigil and discovered the true meaning of the term "pitch black." I have never investigated in an area so dark. My hand could not be seen just inches from my face. The area became active very quickly—with more energy than I had experienced on any other investigation. I stood in the middle of the room and witnessed a string of light anomalies, one after the other, circle menacingly—as though I was the one being investigated. I started to see shadows darting around the room, and stones and dirt from the floor began pinging off the wall like ricocheting bullets. A large stone then appeared on the floor in front of me—that was not there when I started the vigil! The electricity in the room was incredible, and I gripped my video recorder firmly and panned around the room. I braced myself and waited to see what would arrive—it was tense.

During this encounter I kept a DVR running and conducted a commentary as each new light or shadow presented itself; after twenty minutes of concentrated action the atmosphere changed and became calm. I looked back through the video footage and could clearly see the circling light anomalies accompanied by the noise of the bouncing stones. During the course of the vigil I had asked, "Do you have a name?"

I never heard a response to my question at the time, but I managed to record an answer on both my video recorder and DVR, which I listened to afterwards during the evidence review. It said, in a female voice, as clear as you would hear me talking next to you, "Carrie!" Due to the strength of this EVP I decided to venture down once more to try and gain further contact with Carrie. I did a prolonged twelve-minute sweep with the DVR and proceeded to record nine more EVPs. In the gaps left for a response to my questions, I heard, "Fuck you" and "Fuck off," retorted in a gravelly male voice. It was chilling for me to play this back and hear the vitriolic aggression in the voice.

The story of the basement does not end here. I was present during a recent series of vigils with another team and witnessed the violent assault of a female investigator—she was grabbed aggressively by the throat and thrown to the ground. When we ascended to the sanctuary of the light we discovered fresh scratch marks flailed deep across her back—as though somebody had brought the back of their hands together over her spine and clawed her outwards towards the waist. As she could not have caused the scratches herself, I cannot rationalize an explanation for this event, other than labeling it paranormal. Our pastor, Steve H., commented that the scratch marks were in groups of three, suggesting that the entity had only three fingers on each hand. He also claimed that this may have been a mocking of the Holy Trinity.

Conclusion

The most important aspect of the evidence retrieved from the theater is the corroboration of our equipment with the information gained from the interviews. The names received via the ghost box were unknown to the team and were only verified after the vigil by past patrons—this was an investigation where history, psychics, and equipment all worked in unison. The sighting of the ghost in the lobby and the physical assault in the basement also provide chilling evidence to suggest that the Mounds Theatre is haunted.

The Mounds Theatre has now been eaten up by the modernity, noise, and congestion of twenty-first-century east St. Paul—with its street life, bars, and twenty-four-hour shops. But this small, almost unnoticeable building nestled between the conurbation of housing and intersections could be the last quiet refuge for the town's ghosts and spirits—a place they can frequent in death as they did in life. It would not be unreasonable to suggest that as you sit down to watch your next play or film that you are in turn being watched by those who haven't paid for a ticket.

CHAPTER 4

Fort Snelling

St. Paul

Furniture that moves around, a phantom black dog, and an entire ghost army suggest that you are safer outside of the fort than in.

The investigation at Fort Snelling took place during a single day with the fort historian as our guide (we had previously undertaken a day of baseline tests). My research was led by the firsthand accounts of employees who had worked at the fort over many years; I also expanded the information displayed within the fort museum by using period newspaper articles accessed from the Minnesota Historical Society. The many published texts and papers outlining the fort's history also proved valuable.

Colonel Snelling's residence, built in 1822

HISTORY

Fort Snelling is a reminder of America's ambition to place a stronghold in what was then called the Northwest; it represents a monumental symbol of expansion and protection in what was the middle of an untamed wilderness (a sparsely inhabited stretch of uncharted land reached out beyond the fort). The fortification was constructed primarily to protect U.S. interests from the perceived threat of British and Canadian forces from the north, and from American Indians still loyal to British ideologies. This brief also included denying non-U.S. citizens access to the trade routes via the rivers (this area was sporadically populated by foreign fur traders), promoting peace between the Ojibwe and the Dakota Sioux, and stopping white settlers from encroaching onto the land until treaties could be ratified. The fort also became a focal point

for Native Americans to trade and discuss government poli-
cies, and as a site for celebrations and sports.

Lt. Zebulon Pike originally purchased the land in 1805—
it was a perfect location for a fort due to the way it fell into
the natural confluence of the Mississippi and Minnesota
rivers. The Dakota Sioux also saw the geographical importance of the land and revered it as a sacred place of origin,
due to the meeting of the two rivers—they referred to the
area as B'Dote. Building work could not commence though
until political events fell into place; after the war of 1812
the development of Indian agencies throughout the Northwest frontier enabled a support network that acted as a catalyst for construction—this started on the fort in 1820 when
the foundations were put in place. Colonel Josiah Snelling
(1782–1828) designed the floor plan in the shape of an elon-
gated diamond; to the west he placed a large tower complete
with gun holes and a canon, to the east was built a half-moon-
shaped battery. The soldiers were solely responsible for the
fort's construction, and they resided a mile from the site at
Camp Coldwater during the building process.

The fort was finally completed in 1824 and was given a
new name in honor of the colonel (it was originally conceived
as Fort St. Anthony). The scale of Fort Snelling was in stark
contrast to normal military procedure—other fortifications
tended to be temporary. The fort reflected a statement of
intent towards America's plans for expansion and highlighted
the isolation of the site—there would be no reinforcements
coming if the fort ever came under attack. As soldiers edged
their way into the wilderness, it was normal military policy to

create small fortifications as they went; they would then progress farther from that site and set up the next camp.

This policy came to fruition in 1851 when new treaties
opened the territory of Minnesota to settlement; the cities of
St. Paul and Minneapolis soon became firmly established and
the need for a forward frontier military post was gone. This
also coincided with the building of newer forts further north
and west. Fort Snelling subsequently became redundant and
evolved into nothing more than a storage depot.

INVESTIGATION

Poltergeist Activity in the Snelling House

I walked towards the fort entrance with the bright red, white,
and blue Stars and Stripes above my head—it stood out viv-
idly against the turquoise sky and flapped eagerly at the top
of the west turret. I was met by a fort employee resplendent
in a full military uniform from the mid-nineteenth century,
with white breeches and a red tunic. He held an overly long
musket upright against his shoulder. The reason for the fort's
existence was to emphasize a claim to the land and to keep
out the British, but on this occasion I just walked through
the entrance unchallenged.

I started our exploration in Colonel Snelling's living
quarters; this gave me the opportunity to investigate the oldest residential building in the state of Minnesota. If spirits
or ghosts were to be found at Fort Snelling, this would be
the place to find them. The house was constructed in 1822,
and like much of the fort was built from local limestone and
white pine cut from the surrounding forests. The house has a
ground level with a large drawing room, a dining room, and

two bedrooms. A staircase ascends to the attic rooms, each of which has a bed and exposed sloping timber roofs, making it impossible for anyone tall to access the edges. The lack of light in this area promotes a feeling of claustrophobia. Most rooms are sparsely furnished in antique period furniture (apart from the ground-floor bedrooms). A stairwell leads down to the basement level, where four smaller rooms can be found—the kitchen, quartermaster's office, storeroom, and cook's bedroom.

A fort employee, dressed in a bonnet and period costume, had experienced what she believed to be paranormal activity in the house; she described how she securely locks the interior and exterior doors of the house at the end of the day before she leaves. On several occasions she had arrived the following morning to discover all of the doors open and the furniture rearranged. It is difficult to believe this could be the work of a nonparanormal trickster—especially as a breach of the fort would be required to achieve this.

During the Snellings' residence, a wounded Dakota Indian was rushed into the fort; medical facilities were at best limited, and any serious injuries would be almost impossible to treat. The Indian was instantly recognized as a trusted friend of the Snelling family; without hesitation he was brought into the house to be afforded the most comfort and care—he was hospitalized in the Snellings' bedroom. This brutal and lawless society (the soldiers were trying to police) saw many territorial conflicts between individual tribes as well as the encroaching white man; this would often result in the death or injury of Native Americans, trappers, soldiers, and local citizenry. Abigail Hunt Snelling, the colonel's second wife, kept a vigil by the Indian's bedside—attending to his needs until the man died. It is possible the Indian's slow and painful death imprinted paranormal energy into the house—this could be responsible for the furniture moving around at night.

Spirits of a Mother and Child

When we first entered the house, Lisa saw the spirit of a child; when he became aware that he could be seen, he ran upstairs—we followed him to the top-floor bedrooms. Lisa walked around the bed into the far corner of the room and stooped down to avoid hitting her head on the beams. After a short dialogue, directed into the seemingly empty semidarkness, she informed us that two spirits were present—their names were Joe and Victoria. Joe was the little boy she had seen running and he was sitting next to Victoria, his mother. Joe was a common name during this period, but it is worth mentioning that Colonel Snelling's son was named Joseph and would have resided in the house. Joseph was described by his teacher John Marsh, when he taught the fort children in 1823: "'Joe' was wayward, wild, adventurous, and red-haired."[19]

I decided to make further contact by using the Ovilus—for recording purposes I had a DVR and a digital infrared camera running while I tried to engage in conversation. I started by asking the question, "Where are we?"

The electronic voice came through instantaneously: "Snell."

Then just as quickly it said, "Mutt."

The spirit of a child ran up the stairwell of the Snelling residence

Snell is not one of the words programmed into the machine
—I thought it may have tried to say *Snelling*, but had fallen
short. I then decided to do a DVR sweep to see what more I
could ascertain. I asked if anyone was present, and the reply
came back as, "Yes."

This response was not heard by any members of the team
(many of the replies we get are inaudible at the time but are
subsequently picked up after analyzing our recorded data in
the evidence review). So I asked the same question again without realizing I had already received a reply—the response this
time was audible in the room.

"Aye."

This word is a historical military term used as an affirma-
tive; it is also used in Celtic countries as a colloquial word for
yes—it is certainly not unusual for entities to engage with
us in the vernacular of the period they are from. The fort
has a long history of Irish and Scottish settlers working and
residing there as well as being a melting pot for many other
nationalities; Irish and Scottish immigrants (from Lord Sel-
kirk's unsuccessful colony in Canada) were given temporary
shelter in the fort, so would have frequented the area in considerable numbers. The fort was also a transient refuge for
army officers, government officials, and an increasing number of eastern tourists who would have stopped at the fort for
lodgings and supplies.

The Irish and Scottish immigrants were also joined by
a large number of French and Swiss nationals. In 1839 this
multinational settlement was forced by the Army to move
further down the river; they formed a small hamlet that
eventually grew into the city of St. Paul. Other settlements

were also seeing a growth in population as a result of the fort; the American and Columbia fur companies built their headquarters nearby. As all traders were required to have their goods inspected at the fort, their employees settled in nearby Mendota.

I considered that the initial word of *snell* may have been the German word for *quick* (*schnell* in modern Standard German). In this context, "mutt" could then be seen as a shortening of the word *Mutter*, or "mother," in the same way Americans shorten *mother* to *Mom*—thus producing the phrase "quick mother." The Swiss immigrants would have spoken German, and I already knew that a mother and child were present in the attic room—could this have been a warning that Joseph was trying to give his mother upon our arrival?

The majority of the paranormal phenomena we documented or were informed about took place during the day, in bright sunlight. Paranormal activity is just as prevalent during the day as it is at night; the reason most investigations take place during the night is due to other factors. Many of the buildings I investigate have public access throughout the day, so a late-night investigation usually provides me with the best opportunity for collecting evidence—which cannot be contaminated by people walking and talking in the vicinity (outside noise pollution from cars is also reduced). Many paranormal experiences are also nonvisual; we have a greater, heightened awareness of smells and sounds when we are deprived of our visual sense. Finally, if an entity is trying to manifest itself and is only capable of producing a faint light emission, it is more likely to be recognized and witnessed in a dark environment, as it does not have to compete with the surrounding ambient light to be seen.

The Phantom Black Dog

A member of the staff sat resplendently in a period dress and apron, complete with a hat, directing visitors outside the main barracks. She told me her daughter used to play in the fort during the school holidays—her daughter is now fully grown and is also a fort employee. She recently asked her mother about the mysterious black dog she saw as a child (she remembers that it used to run freely around the fort, appearing suddenly, before vanishing again). Her mother informed her that no dog had ever been present in the fort—certainly not in the time she had worked there. Other employees were subsequently asked whether they remembered seeing a black dog wandering around the fort—not a single person had seen the animal. The fort is completely secure so no dog could have penetrated the interior by accident; the surrounding site is also difficult to access as it is positioned between two rivers and the bluffs—it is also some distance from the nearest conurbation. It could then be argued that the young girl experienced a paranormal encounter.

Supernatural black dogs or hellhounds are common in paranormal mythology and fiction—there are stories of canine apparitions reported from every corner of the globe. The oldest written documentation of a black-dog legend dates back to 1190, in Walter Map's book *De nugis curialium*. These tales have been embellished over the centuries and mixed with Native American traditions and the folklore of German, Dutch, and Scandinavian settlers. There are many accounts of hellhounds behaving benevolently (like the one witnessed in the fort) throughout the United States as early as the nineteenth century. Sightings of benign canine apparitions have been documented in Hanging Hills in Connecticut; Adamstown in Lancaster County, Pennsylvania; and in Warfieldsburg, Carroll County, Maryland.

Dogs have always had a close association with fighting and the supernatural; during the English Civil War, Prince Rupert took his large poodle dog, "Boye," into battle with him. The dog was greatly feared on the battlefield and was believed to be a familiar with paranormal powers. The dog was eventually killed during the Battle of Marston Moor in 1644, allegedly shot through the heart with a silver bullet.

The sightings of hellhounds describe many of the same features and characteristics: they have black fur, make no sound, leave no footprints, and have the ghostly characteristics of suddenly appearing and disappearing (exactly how the fort dog behaved and looked). In many cultures it is thought that a hellhound symbolizes a bad omen or an imminent death; it is believed that if you see a hellhound and speak about the experience before a year and a day has passed, you will come to an untimely death. Luckily and unknowingly, the young fort worker did not speak of her interaction with the black dog until she reached adulthood. Hellhounds are often assigned to guard the entrances to the world of the dead, such as graveyards, burial grounds, ancient pathways, and sites where executions have taken place; they can also undertake other duties related to the afterlife—like hunting down lost souls.

Native American Executions

The belief that hellhounds are seen on sites associated with death and executions led me to investigate the darker side of Fort Snelling's past. During the harsh winter of 1862–63, approximately 1,700 Dakota Indians—mostly elders, women, and children—were incarcerated in a concentration camp on Pike Island (at Fort Snelling). They arrived there after what was called the *Dakota Death March* of November 1862, arriving from the Lower Sioux Agency in southern Minnesota during the aftermath of the Dakota War.

Several hundred of the Indians died from disease and starvation during this forced captivity. The fort was then used in December 1862 to imprison a large number of Dakota Indians who were awaiting trial for the crimes of murder and rape committed during the Dakota War; after the trial, thirty-eight men were hanged together in Mankato—in what was the largest mass execution in American history. Two Dakota leaders, Chief Shakopee (Little Six) and Wakanozhanzhan (Medicine Bottle), managed to evade capture and escaped north to Canada. Unfortunately, they were betrayed, captured, drugged, and sent back to Fort Snelling, where they were hanged outside of the fort walls on November 11, 1865.

Deaths and executions continued into the twentieth century, when George S. Knapp was executed in Bastrop, Texas, for crimes committed during the Second World War; his body was then flown back to Minnesota and buried at Fort Snelling (the U.S. Military executed 141 of its own servicemen for crimes committed between 1942 and 1945).

The West Turret

The fort was never used in a combat situation, but it was evident that a hellhound would have every reason to frequent the site. Based on this information, I revisited the evidence I captured in the upstairs bedroom of the colonel's house—when the Ovilus gave me the word *mutt*, I wondered if this had any relevance to the black-dog story. I then proceeded to the west turret and decided to use the Ovilus again, based on the positive results I had previously achieved. I had barely turned on the device when three words were said to me in quick succession:

"Bark—dog—mutt."

These were the only three words that came out of the Ovilus at this time. The team agreed that this was an interesting piece of evidence, due to its canine theme—especially as the story of the hellhound was still fresh in our memories. It is also worth noting that when the fort first came into operation it neighbored a Dakota Sioux Indian village. This encampment was three miles farther down the Minnesota River and was the dwelling of Chief Big Eagle—the village was called "Black Dog."

The Ghost Soldier

There have been a number of ghost-soldier sightings by staff and public alike; one of the most prominent incidents took place during a reenactment, when enthusiasts had gathered for a day of celebration and historical fun. At the end of the proceedings, when everyone had returned to their twenty-first-century clothing, a participant walked into the hospital barracks. As he was entering the building, a soldier in full military uniform walked past him. The reenactor did not recognize the soldier—which he thought unusual as he knew all of the actors who had participated in the event. The soldier appeared steely-faced and showed little emotion as he passed the man in the narrow corridor. The man felt uneasy about the brief encounter and thought there was something odd about the soldier; he turned around to take a second look but discovered the soldier had vanished. The reenactor was known to be a very honest person, and his story is reinforced by many other sightings of a soldier in this location.

Soldier Deaths

No military action ever took place at the fort, but I wanted to discover if any soldiers had still lost their lives here in order to facilitate a haunting; the life of a Minnesota fort soldier was harsh, and death was never far away. The positioning of the fort magnifies the Minnesota seasons; it intensifies the strong summer sun, which reflects off the bleached, aridly dry limestone walls—causing you to squint into the dust bowl of a parade ground. The winters are bitterly cold, and the wind whistles down the Mississippi bringing both snow and ice; this, I discovered, claimed the lives (after their bodily extremities) of many loyal soldiers who stood on sentry duty in subzero temperatures. The soldiers suffered greatly from hypothermia and severe frostbite through the wearing of ineffectual clothing. This severe climate was recognized in the *Minneapolis Journal* on November 5, 1901, as the U.S. Army's continued use of Fort Snelling was being debated—even during this period a threat from Canada was still perceived:

Some authorities hold that Fort Snelling is in too cold a climate to be made one of the central bases of the army. Evidently the authorities expect that our soldiers will never have to campaign in a cold climate. We hope not, but one of the two foreign countries whose soil touches ours lies north of the forty-ninth parallel.[20]

Other fatalities were caused by sledding, hunting, firearms incidents, drowning, and disease; even as late as the beginning of the twentieth century the poor sanitation was being highlighted as a cause for concern for illness and disease:

Major Philip Reade, inspector general of the Department of Dakota, in his annual report to General Otis and the war department, lays special stress upon the unsanitary conditions of the plumbing and defective drainage of the barracks at Fort Snelling, and especially in the quarters known as "Minnesota Row."[21]

Sickness amongst soldiers was far worse in other forts and military encampments, however. Early in the fort's history it was beginning to be known that fresh fruit and vegetables played an important role in a soldier's diet, in trying to avoid illness, so the forward-thinking Colonel Snelling started farming in and around the fort as soon as the construction started. Post commanders were placed in charge of gardens, and cultivation soon took over fort duties in the absence of conflict. Potatoes and wheat were the first crops to be harvested on the initial ninety-acre site. By 1823 over one hundred acres of wheat was being sown with another one hundred acres utilized for other produce—over one hundred barrels of flour were produced that year. The government also had a reputation for delivering food supplies that were often rotten or unpalatable, as well as for delivering emaciated livestock. In 1821 the government also stopped paying for seed supplies, which made self-sufficiency more of a necessity. Weather played an integral part of fort life, with supplies and a soldier's well-being linked to its fickle nature; thus, observations were noted by the fort's doctor from January 1820 onwards, giving the Twin Cities one of the most comprehensive historical weather records in the country.

Colonel Snelling himself became sick and was given a combination of opium and brandy by the camp doctor as medication—which had the effect of exacerbating his alcoholism. It was said that Snelling was a reasonable commander when he was sober but was susceptible to angry, alcohol-fueled outbursts. He was recalled to Washington, D.C., due to his ill health in the fall of 1827 and died the following summer of chronic dysentery and "brain fever."

I took Lisa onto the parade ground to see if she could see our ghostly soldier incumbent—this was to provide her with one of her most profound paranormal encounters.

Army of the Dead

Every hour the fort employees perform a drill in the parade ground wearing full nineteenth-century military uniforms, for the benefit of the tourists and visitors. The sergeant barks out orders and a handful of soldiers follow his commands in unison, gun in hand, working their way through a series of choreographed moves. What Lisa witnessed was an emotional encounter with an entire ghost army of soldiers. They stood with the actors and staff in lines several rows deep, following the same orders from the sergeant, moving in perfect unison in time with the living soldiers. Lisa was visibly choked up. The fort employees were completely unaware that standing amongst their ranks was an entire army of the dead—still feeling it was their duty, even in the afterlife, to fulfill their obligation to protect the fort and to follow the commands of a senior officer.

This was one occasion when the differences between a residual haunting and an intelligent haunting become blurred. The clockwork regularity of the hourly drill would suggest a haunting that is replayed at a specific time and place. A sentry's life of metronomic routines could easily see a disembodied spirit return to the same place it frequented in life, over and over again. Yet the ghosts are responding to the drill sergeant, so an intelligent response is taking place out on the bleached, dried earth. This was an army of ghosts standing side by side on the parade ground following the same orders and wearing the same uniform—split by the chasm of 188 years, but brought seamlessly together with the living.

CONCLUSION

The firsthand accounts of employees, reinforced by our equipment and psychic work, would suggest the fort is active—but a further, prolonged investigation of the fort would be required. I did not personally see the paranormal soldiers, and the recorded data was solely reflective of the families and civilians that were also residing there. The black-dog theme is highly significant though and is backed up with historical knowledge, firsthand primary source material taken from the interviews, and the corroboration of two separate pieces of investigative equipment in two separate areas. This would suggest that someone or something followed us around or was omnipresent—as well as wanted to communicate information to us. At a future investigation I would want to leave a dog-related trigger object at the fort (a bone, for example) with a static night-vision camera to pan the parade ground; I would also like to use a series of DVRs in the hope of recording dog noises.

Soldiering is a vocation based on loyalty, dedication, routine, patriotism, comradeship, and a sense of pride. These are surely the humanistic qualities one would need above all others to guarantee that a ghost continues to frequent a site, long after the body had disappeared. I do not know if the dead army knew they were dead or whether it was just another day of following orders at Fort Snelling, but Lisa left the soldiers on the parade ground that day, under the bright fluttering Stars and Stripes, with tears rolling down her face.

CHAPTER 5

The Soap Factory Building

MINNEAPOLIS

This location is one of the most paranormally thick environments I have ever had the displeasure to investigate; the death and rendering down of animal carcasses have left a dark, menacing presence at the Soap Factory.

I had the opportunity of undertaking three visits to the Soap Factory building over the last two years; the evidence that follows is a culmination of those investigations. My team originally asked executive director Ben Heywood to investigate the property after he and other members of his staff had experienced paranormal activity. The building is currently used as a space for artistic experimentation and innovation, dedicated to supporting artists and engaging audiences through the production and presentation of contemporary art. The Soap Factory organization supports artists and their work by not only providing exhibition and studio space on an unprecedented scale, but also by providing skilled staff to aid artists in realizing new work.

A large contribution to my research on the factory was undertaken via the Internet; there are a growing number of sites that allow you access to period newspapers and documents online—this supplemented the traditional research methods I undertook at the local historical society. I also interviewed Ben about the processes of soap-making and the history of the building and surrounding area. He provided me with valuable documents that focused my research. Many of the businesses that are mentioned in the chapter have their own websites outlining their history. Documents detailing immigration details are also widely available online.

HISTORY

The Soap Factory building is the oldest unconverted warehouse space on the Minneapolis riverfront. Built in 1883, this cavernous cathedral of a space sits uniquely in the middle of the old milling district of the Marcy-Holmes neighborhood—next to the Pillsbury A Mill; its derelict surroundings are now the only reminder of the era when Minneapolis was the flour-milling capital of the world. Its interior has been stripped bare now, but it still shows the scars of a history of transformation and adaptation—and the industrial-scale rendering process that saw animal carcasses turned into soap.

The Union Railway Storage Company (URSC) originally built and operated the 66' x 100' warehouse; the one-story building was used primarily for the storage of lime, cement, and other building supplies. Access and transportation of the materials were facilitated by the railroad track that ran alongside the southwest of the property; a further two stories were added in 1892 as the URSC continued to utilize the building up until 1915.

JELLY PRODUCTION

The Grant Storage Battery Company then took charge of the warehouse before modifications and additions were added in 1917. As the building readied itself for the newly evolving market of jelly production, the Wheeler-Barnes Company (manufacturer of syrups, preserves, and peanut butter) and the Home Foods Jelly Factory moved onto the site. Strangely, the American market for jelly evolved from the First World War; grape jam was patented by Paul Welch in 1917 for the puréeing of grapes—his entire product (which he called Grapelade) was then purchased on mass by the U.S. Army and exported to troops in France on the frontline. When the combatants finally returned home, they created a consumer market for the product from the taste they acquired for it overseas (60,000 First World War troops came from Minnesota); grape jam and other variants were put into large-scale production, and the factory was expanded again in the early 1920s to handle the volume of production.

THE NEED FOR SOAP

The URSC ran their operations in the 1880s on a timeline parallel to the growing market for soap manufacture in the Minneapolis area. The demand for soap-based products during this era was due to an increase in dirty industrial manual labor and the growing fashion for scented bathroom soaps;

this added to an already buoyant market (created from the new awareness that cleanliness helped stop the spread of germs and diseases).

The Twin Cities were at the center of soap production in the 1880s, and many factories began to spring up along the banks of the Mississippi. The advantages were outlined in an article from 1884:

> Tallow can be purchased here at a lower price than anywhere else in the United States, and the rosin which is used in the soap boiling is cheapened by river transportation. The chemicals used are brought from Europe, but they are shipped in concentrated form and the freight charges do not figure conspicuously.[22]

Soap prices began to rise dramatically due to demand outstripping supply; this placed prominent soap manufacturers in a very healthy financial position.

A History of Ghosts

The process of soap-making in Minneapolis, even during this early period, was interwoven with tales of the supernatural; an article written in the *Minneapolis Journal* on March 27, 1901, not only documents the manifestation of an apparition, but allows us to recognize the unique combination of a disused factory and the process of soap-making as conducive to paranormal activity:

> The Soap House Ghost: The old Bradshaw soap building on the First Avenue car line where it crosses the Chicago, Milwaukee, & St. Paul tracks, at Twenty-

Ninth Street, is accused of being haunted. The old building has not been used for several years as a soap factory, and its emphasis has tended to the rapid development of any ghost germs which might have escaped the action of the lye used in the soap manufacture. It is not known if cold or warmth is necessary to the propagation of the shades that infest the building, but at any rate the past winter has been conductive to their growth, for the other evening as a young man passed the building he heard a rattling of the window bars. Looking up he saw a sight which he "will never forget" until he joins the Buffaloes. Standing back from the windows a short distance stood a wondrously large man enveloped in a green vapor. His face was like the label put on cigarette boxes in South Dakota, the skull and crossbones. His cheekbones were very protuberant and from his eye sockets issued an illuminated green mist. When he had broken the spell by force of will, the young man ran.

The scientists that have been asked concerning the apparition say that it is a seeming appearance caused by the exhalation of fumes of surgeon's green soap which has not yet evaporated from the vats.[23]

In historical literature and poetry, a "shade" is a ghost or spirit that is residing in the underworld. In biblical Hebrew, the term *tsalmaveth* literally means "death-shadow" and is used to describe the dead that are trapped in the shadow of hell. In the first Book of Samuel, the Witch of Endor conjures the shade or ghost of Samuel. Only a chosen few are exempt from the fate of dwelling in the purgatory of the shadows, before ascending to the divine. Outside of biblical literature, shades appear in Homer's *The Odyssey*, when Odysseus sees them in a vision of Hades, and in Dante's *Divine Comedy*, when Virgil and the dead are referred to as shades.

Even in 1901 scientists were trying to explain away paranormal phenomena; it remains unclear though how a pedestrian standing outside could succumb to the fumes said to be emanating from inside a long-since-disused factory—it would also be highly unlikely that any lye and fat residues left in the vats would evaporate so easily. The hypothesis that the swirling green mist was caused by the crushed-fuchsite mica mineral that gives surgical potassium soap its color would also be difficult to believe, as that is a ground mineral and not a gas.

THE NATIONAL PURITY SOAP COMPANY

In 1924 the Leifgren family took over the factory and introduced soap production, bringing with them a more industrialized approach; they founded the National Purity Soap Company and began to manufacture kettle-boiled tallow soap on the site. This was a time when most small Midwestern towns had at least one community dairy, and National Purity made soaps and detergents for the dairy and creamery business. Farmers and dairy owners bought National Purity products in order to clean milking equipment, milk trucks, bottles, pails, containers, barn doors, and even cows. It was a cyclical process that saw cattle turned into soap to help keep the dairy industry sterile and clean.

By 1992 the original nineteenth-century-built factory was outdated and inefficient, so National Purity decided to relocate to expand manufacturing facilities west of downtown Minneapolis. The factory remained empty until 1995, when a nonprofit art gallery, aimed towards the young emerging contemporary artists of Minneapolis, moved into the space.

NEGATIVE ENERGY DUE TO LOCATION

The history of this part of Minneapolis is layered like the decades of ground-in soap. Several years before the warehouse/factory was built, a small manufacturing business started up in the district; it produced artificial limbs primarily for soldiers wounded during the Civil War. Before the war artificial-limb companies barely existed, and anyone who was unlucky enough to lose a limb had to make do or fashion a device that worked for them—with the aid of a local carpenter or blacksmith. An amputee's main priority was to carry on working to support themselves and their family; any financial help would only come from the church or wealthy philanthropists—no welfare program existed.

Most businesses were created by the individuals who fashioned a prosthetic arm or leg for themselves and saw the benefit of running a limb company to sell to others. A. A. Winkley was one such entrepreneur; he was a horse farmer from Minnesota who developed a prosthetic leg for himself. With private backing he formed the Winkley Company in 1889 just prior to a national Civil War veterans' reunion in Minneapolis. His designs were immediately popular with veterans, becoming the catalyst for a successful business that is still operational today. This made the area a center for pained and injured veterans traveling from all over Minnesota to be fitted with artificial limbs—bringing with them suffering and anguish. The possibility of residual negative energy was something we considered before we started to investigate.

THE SLAUGHTER OF ANIMALS

It is believed that the animal carcasses used here in the soap-making process were slaughtered offsite during the period of the National Purity years. Before the end of the nineteenth century, without an infrastructure of transportation, it would have been easier to walk the animals straight into a factory to be slaughtered—close to where they would be needed. Whether they were slaughtered on this site or not, it is probable that the factory is paranormally active due to the continual stream of dead animals that were processed here—over a prolonged period of time.

As we went about our vigils it was interesting to note that the whole team felt as though they were being watched, almost circled at times. These presences always lingered in the shadows and refused to engage with us in the ways we would have wanted; they seemed nervous and untrusting. It was exactly the kind of behavior you would expect to see from an animal. The random noises, bangs, and crashes throughout the building and the scuffling and moving around could have been from living animals like rats and pigeons of course, but we never saw either of these animals at any time we were in the factory. I decided to research further the suffering of animals on the site and discovered that large numbers of dogs were killed and disposed of at the gates of soap factories all over the city.

As Minneapolis grew in the later years of the nineteenth century, its population of stray and unlicensed dogs rose to alarming rates. In 1898 it was believed that a staggering 35,000 dogs roamed the city. This increase led local authorities to pay one dollar for every dog that was captured and removed from the streets. This became a catalyst for many unregulated, unscrupulous individuals to take up the position of dog catcher in an attempt to make a living.

The dog catcher would wear a tin star to highlight his identity and trade as he went about stalking the shadows of the warehouses of the Mississippi—stealthily skulking and prowling premises, armed with his snares and cudgel (listening intently for a misplaced bark or whimper). The dog catcher employed a loose team of "spotters" to roam the back streets and alleyways looking for any canine that did not carry the brass tag around its neck that would serve as a passport to its freedom. The scene of a dog catcher moving through the city at this time was described by the *Daily Globe* of St. Paul on September 6, 1885:

> What can make an entire family madder than to see their pet Fido caught with a treacherous snare, thrown unceremoniously into a rickety old cart and then drawn off, behind the scarecrow of a horse, to be locked up in an ugly, foreboding dog pound.[24]

An air of mystery surrounded the way in which the dog catcher would skillfully capture his prey, gaining the dog's confidence in order to apprehend the animal without being bitten. One very observant small boy, residing on 10th Street, offered a child's explanation as to how one dog catcher could be so effective in grabbing a mutt:

> The dog catcher has five fingers on each hand, and there must be something about those two extra fingers that can get in on our dog.[25]

This particular dog catcher had polydactylism, a birth condition that results in having five fingers and one thumb on each hand, leading the children of Minneapolis to cruelly call out "five-fingered Jack" whenever he went by.

Despite the dog catcher's disheveled appearance, his vocation was deceptively profitable; one of the city's first official dog catchers was George Bevers, whose accounts were published in the *Daily Globe* in 1888. From the beginning of his employment on May 1 until October 22 of that year he made the sum of $2000, a considerable amount of money during this era; this amount represented the capture of 1,400 dogs at an average of eight dogs per day.

For those unlucky canines that were not reclaimed within three days, a further profit could be made by selling their fur to the local tanneries and their carcasses to a soap factory—rare-breed dogs could also be sold to willing recipients for a profit. Accusations of nabbing expensive dogs that were legally owned or tethered, in order to financially benefit from their sale in the illegal black market, saw many dog catchers removed from their positions and fined in a court of law.

In 1898 a more professional approach was undertaken by the local authorities, when they looked to employ dog catchers on a flat rate rather than the previous payment method based on the number of dogs caught—this was announced in the *Daily Globe* on July 15 of that year:

> The matter came before the committee on the resolution authorizing the mayor to appoint six dog catchers at $50 a month and five men with teams and wagons at $3 a day to collect licenses and gather in the unlicensed canines.[26]

Although the job had many financial benefits, it could be detrimental to the dog catcher's social standing:

> While there is a great amount of financial satisfaction connected with the office of city dog catcher, the position has its drawbacks, for after a man has once accepted the position he is ostracized from all select society. He is set down as a pirate on general principles, and the vast legion of dog owners hate him with a whole hearted hatred that no amount of time can heal.[27]

Families and neighborhoods could become aggressive if they witnessed their beloved pet apprehended. On one occasion a policeman had to step in to protect a dog catcher from being seriously hurt, as an unruly mob showered him with stones as he tried to make off with a pet.

The effectiveness of the dog catchers, combined with their assiduity for making money, ultimately led to their demise. The dog catchers were eventually reduced in number and made to work seasonally during the warmer months, leaving the remaining dogs to roam the streets of Minneapolis safe in the knowledge that their fur was not going to keep someone else warm the following winter.

INDUSTRIAL ACCIDENTS

The dangerous nature of the soap-making process is still visible; in the gloomy darkness one glimpses emergency showers with ceramic trays and rusted, distressed plumbing ready to douse an unlucky worker who came into violent contact with the boiling fat and burning lye. Eye baths are evident, and warning signs, despite their age and state of dilapidation, still inform the reader of the many dangers that the process posed; the pain and anguish of an industrial accident may have left a paranormal imprint on the fabric of the structure.

There are three main ingredients for making soap—fat, lye, and water; the soap factory probably used rendered cattle, horse, and dog carcasses to obtain the fat (tallow). This created hard soap for use in hot water—the tallow was melted down into a liquid (oil) to use in the process. Lye is an alkaline hydroxide (NaOH)—potassium hydroxide (caustic potash) or sodium hydroxide (caustic soda) are most commonly used. Lye is an extremely corrosive poison and can cause blindness and serious burns to the skin. If drunk it can prove fatal. Water is then added to the lye; the best water to use is soft water, as hard water contains mineral salts that hinder the cleansing action of soap. The factory is in close proximity to the banks of the Mississippi, and it would be reasonable to assume that the river provided a regular supply of water straight into the building.

Saponification is the name given to the chemical reaction when the lye and fat are converted into one substance during the hot-process—this is the soap. The lye and fat are boiled together at 220–275 degrees Fahrenheit, although the soap can get as hot as 330 degrees; this is also dangerous due to its tendency to splutter or ignite if the vat is boiled too vigorously.

The dangers of soap production can be easily seen by the disasters that befell rival soap-making factories in Minneapolis:

> The fire was found to be the Northwestern soap factory, located at the corner of Second Avenue north and Fifth Street, next to Bidwell and Co., pork packers, a very greasy locality. The soap factory was totally destroyed, nothing being saved but one office desk. One of the employers lost everything, even to hat and coat, his trunk and his clothes, and a $98 cornet being in the factory.[28]

> An explosion today in the soap factory of B. McGurri & Sons, Thirty-First Street and Western Avenue, almost completely demolished the plant and injured four persons. The accident was due to a boiling over of a large cauldron of grease.[29]

A cursory glance through the daily newspapers throughout this period of soap production would furnish you with regular tales of explosions, fires, and deaths.

Ben Heywood kindly allowed the team to explore many parts of the Soap Factory building that are closed to the public due to safety concerns; we had to be especially careful walking around in the dark, regardless of paranormal activity. There were missing floorboards, an open elevator shaft that falls through the building into the basement, doors that lead into rooms with no floors and a three-story drop, and all manner of obsolete industrial hardware and piping that litter the rooms ready to assault a careless investigator. When you grab a handrail or touch a wall for support, the greasy residue of soap and animal fat leaves a trace on the fingers and lingers in the nostrils; caked-in raw soap clings to the internal iron skeleton like stalactites in a cave.

It was not paranormal activity, however, that caused me to feel bitterly cold during the investigations; it was the broken windows and drafty warehouse environment during a Minnesota winter's night. What wasn't caused by the wind was the breathing in my ear when nobody was there; this was a shallow, repeated, breathy breeze that makes you think somebody or something is encroaching into your personal space—either curious about who you are and what you are doing in the darkness or in the hope of scaring you away.

INVESTIGATION

The Noise in the Basement

The labyrinth of the basement takes so many unexpected twists and turns that it defies architectural reasoning and leaves you wondering if you will ever find your way out. It is the result of a slow, unplanned evolution of function over form, as each new technological advance stamped its presence on the internal workings of the building. A giant furnace sits in the belly of the basement and was used to heat the vats that were positioned above. Coal still decorates the floor, and the dust makes a gritty sound under your feet as you trace your way around. The furnace's immense body swells and fills the room, requiring you to edge along the walls in order to navigate it. It was difficult to decide if shoveling the lung-busting coals into the mouth of the furnace in the ambient temperature of an oven in hot weather would be a worse job than being a floor above, mixing the boiling, caustic fat and lye, with all the smells and dangers that entails. History does not give us an insight into the smells of a bygone industrial process, but I know it would have been chokingly bad.

The dust and dirt of a disused factory can easily be kicked into the air with the locomotion of investigators treading on the stairs and floors, especially in areas that have not been accessed for decades. This action created a whole series of photographs that contained what some investigators would call orbs or light anomalies. I believe that light anomalies exist because I have witnessed them—one experience in the basement of the Palmer House Hotel had me wading through them as though I were knee-deep in Christmas lights, but the majority of photographs taken with a flash in these circumstances show dust particles bouncing the flash light back to the camera (small insects, breath, light rain, and water vapor can also cause this effect).

If entities have their own energy, they should be easily seen in a dark environment without the aid of a camera flash to make them visible. Because dust particles cannot usually be seen with the naked eye, they are dismissed as the reason for these images, but if you have witnessed the dust floating around in the bright beam of a film projector or the sun shining into a dimly lit room through a chink in the drapes, then you will be aware of the considerable number of dust particles that surround us. It has been used as an argument that some of the orbs appear to be very large compared to the people or objects in the photographs, so they cannot be tiny dust particles, but this is an effect caused by the particles being closer to the lens when the picture was taken—as objects closer to you appear bigger than those farther away. If you need further convincing, just turn the lights out in your home, thump your sofa, and start taking photographs.

We stood around the furnace, peering into the darkness, and started our vigil. Instantly our sensitives felt the familiar sensation of what they call "rushing"—this is when an entity comes up close to your face in order to observe or scare you. They did this action to each member of the team, but only the sensitives were able to see their behavior; this encounter was interpreted as a malevolent activity due to its threatening vigor and was not seen as curiosity. I asked the entity if it would make its presence known through a sign or signal, and at that precise moment in direct response to my question, a loud metallic banging sound reverberated around the room—it sounded like someone had taken a hammer and struck one of the large ducts that circumvent the factory.

It was difficult to know the exact location where the percussive sound took place, as the noise had traveled throughout the building's pipe work. We had a second team investigating on the third floor during this incident (they were the only other people in the building); I contacted them on the two-way radio to confirm that the noise had not been created by them, but they had also heard the violent bang and were just as surprised as we were.

Then, as we tried to make sense of our auditory response, a second noise broke our thoughts. It sounded like a large object bouncing and careering down the open elevator shaft—these weren't noises that could be made by a lone pigeon or a nervous rat. We picked our way back to the base of the elevator shaft to see what could have caused the noise—these kinds of events should not be happening in a deserted building.

Photographing a Ghost

As we had felt a presence come into the furnace room just before we left, I decided to take a number of photographs to see if I could capture an image of the entity. I set my digital camera up on a tripod and placed it against the wall so it looked into the room. I then took six pictures with a remote shutter release with differing light settings; I did not use a flash as I was aware of the inherent problems of using artificial light as previously discussed. The room was so dark that I could barely see anything in front of me, so long exposures were used to highlight the detail in this location; the investigators were still in the corridor, so the room was completely empty.

The third of the six photographs I had taken revealed an image so incredible that it defies any logical explanation. In the left-hand side of the frame a white shape with a definitive sharp outline appears in the shot and is seen to be slowly traveling from left to right—as the long exposure time has captured the movement. Although this shape has a definite edge and depth, it is at the same time see-through, and you can easily make out parts of the furnace through its white, ethereal body.

*A ghost captured in front of the furnace
in the basement of the Soap Factory*

I would just like to emphasize again that the room was empty, and I took the pictures because we had felt something negative entering the space. There was no flash or any reflective surfaces in the room—the area was almost devoid of light, and the glowing illumination towards the top right of the photograph was created by a small crack in a boarded-up window that appears brighter due to the long exposure time. The ghostly image did not appear on the other five pictures taken from the same spot, at the same time, and from the same angle.

When Spirits Call Out Your Name

I always find it disturbing when the ghost box calls out our names; in the factory we had barely got the equipment running when it spat out several investigators' names. This would suggest that spirits have access to information about us before we investigate (which would require them to have prior knowledge or the ability to interact with other spirits that are close to us—like deceased relatives, friends, or spirit guides—in order to obtain the information). It is also possible that they may hear us chatting before the investigation—this then implies an element of onsite clandestine surveillance, by listening to casual conversations between team members in the building.

Throughout the course of the vigils we kept a constant check on the temperature; one of the tools we use for this is a laser thermometer—it fires a red laser dot onto the surface of an object to register the temperature of the target area. During the top-floor vigil we proceeded to document regular temperature readings; on each occasion the laser beam appeared to be broken by a shadow walking through the beam, which was aimed across the factory floor onto the far side wall. We kept the beam constant to see if this occurrence could be repeated; the beam was broken again several times by the motion of something moving through the light. We then looked extensively in the area with our flashlights, but nothing further was seen—I hoped that our strategically placed DVRs may have recorded an entity in this location.

The Italian Entity

It was during the evidence review of the recorded data from the top floor that a voice came through; it was so loud and clear that it sent shivers running down my spine and made me question why I would ever want to spend my nights in derelict buildings. The voice was male, and it pierced the quiet of the disused factory floor as it said, "Bella luce!"

This phrase is Italian—a language not spoken by any members of the team; it was said in the perfect tone and accent of a native Italian speaker and was clearly not the voice of a team member. Perhaps the very words themselves give us a tantalizing insight into death—*bella luce* means "beautiful light." There is a common theme in the testimony of those who have died and been brought back to life of seeing a beautiful, brilliant white light—as a gateway into the afterlife.

It would not be unusual to hear Italian spoken within the industrial environment of Minneapolis. At the same time the warehouse was first opening its doors at the end of the nineteenth century, the United States was becoming the main destination for Italian immigrants. They arrived at Ellis Island, or "*L'isola delle Lacrime*" (The Island of Tears), before taking the

The Soap Factory, Minneapolis

railroad west to Minnesota; an estimated 78 percent of Italian immigrants at this time were men in their teens and twenties who planned to work in industries like the railroad, construction, and the production of soap.

The First World War severely disrupted immigration from all over Europe, but in the direct aftermath of the fighting it picked up almost immediately. Progressing into the early 1920s, immigration was only limited by the capacity of the liners that kept bringing people over—there was a severe lack of transportation due to wartime losses of shipping. The economy of postwar Italy was so desperate that many Italians looked for a better life abroad; this led to a political internal conflict that eventually brought fascism to the fore in 1922. During the next five years, one and a half million people left Italy; in 1927 the Italian government estimated that 9,200,000 Italians were living abroad—over one-fifth of the entire Italian population at that time.

A Thoughtform

The whole team believed there was something very odd and disconcerting about the Soap Factory building, supported by our experiences. But a psychologist might suggest that it is the prior knowledge you bring with you to a location—an awareness of the processes that took place there. It could also be the influence of the dark architectural semiotics of a gutted, bygone factory. It is a suggested theory that a manifestation could be artificially created through collective negative thoughts; this is known as a thoughtform, or a *tulpa* in Tibetan mysticism. The word *tulpa* is derived from the Sanskrit for "to construct" or "to build."

This energy is manifested consciously or unconsciously through sheer willpower alone—it is a materialized thought that has taken a physical form. The factory generates an income from turning the basement into a haunted-house experience during the Halloween period; this creates the added expectation of being shocked and scared on a mass, collective level—creating an atmosphere of fear within the building for the month of October. It is possible that this environment could be a catalyst for empowering anything negative that is already in the building or is transient and becomes attracted to the projected negativity.

CONCLUSION

The Soap Factory building at night created a feeling of unease deep within the pit of my stomach, a feeling also experienced by other members of the team. This could have been due to a deprivation of vision in the darkness and the deathly quiet—which was only punctuated by paranormal banging. The paranormal activity that I experienced in the factory was certainly disconcerting: it observed me, and it lurked in the shadows and was covert and reluctant to engage—like the defensive and wary standoff-posturing behavioral patterns of a horse or cow. Yet there is also an intelligence that decided to interact with me when I was feeling my most vulnerable—by rushing me, breathing on me, calling my name out, and making loud noises to startle me. Then, in amongst the gloom and darkness, we picked up the most astounding EVP and photograph, challenging us and helping to inform our beliefs. It certainly gives any of us cause to think about what really happens to us after we die.

CHAPTER 6

The Chase Resort

WALKER

A tragic family death and the negative energy from fallen soldiers are in contrast to the beauty and scenery of the Chase on the Lake resort.

When we think of a paranormal environment, our minds tend to race towards graveyards, castles, and damp basements; it is sometimes hard to believe that ghostly activity could be prevalent in an area surrounded by such natural, breathtaking beauty as Leech Lake and the opulent fixtures, fittings, and architectural splendor of the Chase on the Lake resort hotel. But as I soon discovered, beneath the veneer of relaxation and the grounding influence of nature is a meta-narrative of death, violence, and sorrow. It penetrates the surface in the form of mysterious knocking sounds on the hotel doors, unplugged phones ringing in the dead of night, the tread of a ghostly footstep, and the alacrity of a shadow figure glimpsed from the corner of one's eye.

The investigation of the Chase resort hotel in Walker, Cass County, was conducted in a single night—the owner, Steve Olson, and the hotel's management team were very accommodating and allowed me to have full access to the hotel. My research was conducted through employee interviews and archive materials owned by the hotel. Period newspaper articles were accessed online, and various websites expanded my research into the area's history. The Cass County Historical Society museum in Walker also provided me with further information.

HISTORY

The Chase resort on Leech Lake in Walker is situated in an area thick with history and supernatural activity. Some of the oldest human artifacts found in Minnesota have been unearthed in Walker—dating back 15,000 years to the Pleistocene period of the late ice age. This was a time when nomadic man was believed to have entered North America from Asia via a land bridge from Alaska, at a time when Minnesota was a landscape of shifting glaciers; of course where humanity leaves its footprints, paranormal activity usually follows.

Native Americans followed in the path of ice-age man and lived along the pine-covered shores of the lake for many centuries. I believe that much of the paranormal activity in the hotel stems from the conflicts, struggles, and resulting deaths of Native Americans and U.S. soldiers. The first white men to penetrate this area bought pelts from the Native

The Chase on the Lake resort

The Chase on the Lake resort, circa 1922

Americans, and soon fur-trading posts were put in place to facilitate this further. The Minnesota terrain was difficult to traverse, so population growth was very gradual; trails were nothing more than clogged cow paths (in poor weather it was not uncommon for box wagons to be hub-deep in mud).

Walker sits on the western edge of Cass County, and thus many lakes, swamps, and rivers would have to be maneuvered over on the long journey from the Twin Cities. Swamps would be crossed by means of corduroy; these were logs laid close together across the swamps—an attempt was made to cover them, but this soon wore off. To traverse the rivers, early settlers would place their water-tight box wagons upside down and side by side; they were then lashed together with four more wagons placed crossways on top of the first ones. Then a rope was cast across the river, and a person who could swim would make their way across the river and fasten the rope to a tree; the oxen would swim over separately. It was possible for traders to carry more than a thousand pounds of flour over a river in this way without getting it wet.

This method was not without difficulties though, as the wagon wheels and axles contracted and expanded by getting wet and then drying. This caused the wheels to seize up, generating a terrible squeaking noise as the journey continued (the squeaking of the two-wheeled Red River carts would signal the coming of the fur caravans from Canada in the summer). Many of the forts dotted along the path north would keep barrels of bear fat outside the kitchens so that cart axles and wheels could be thoroughly greased before each journey. Many local Indians found themselves on the verge of starvation and would ask the cooking staff to smear the grease on the bread they were given; the grease would contain many dead flies and insects and was usually covered in dirt.

Limited contact with the outside world came via the stagecoach; this was the only means of receiving and conveying mail. Mail in those days was a far more basic means of communication, and in the early days letters were sometimes written on pieces of bark with just charcoal from the fire. This means of transport also proved to be dangerous; stagecoaches were sometimes held up by bands of roving Indians, with the drivers and passengers massacred and the mail left to the four winds. Wolves and other wild animals would make short work of any bodies left in the aftermath of such attacks. The early settlers found that wolves would actually come up to the doors and windows of their cabins at night and howl, especially in the height of winter when food was scarce. Many settlers had to discharge a gun into the cold night air to chase the wolves away.

The expansion of the railroad would come as a relief to settlers venturing north from the Twin Cities, and the fear of Indian attacks, bandits, hazardous river crossings, and wild animals was finally diminished.

A LAWLESS SOCIETY

By the time Cass County was established in 1851, the influx of lumbermen had already begun. That same year the logging entrepreneur Thomas Barlow Walker purchased a large strand of pine in the vicinity, and this rapidly growing community became known as Walker. In an attempt to push through the building of a sawmill, it was hoped that pressure could be placed on Thomas Walker by naming the town after him, thus influencing his decision on where his operations would be located. Disappointingly, he chose nearby Akeley instead. The choice of Akeley over Walker was due to his wife's moral objection to the saloons and brothels that had sprung up in Walker—as witnessed by the Chase family on their arrival two years earlier. This moral objection did not stop others, however, and Walker soon became home to four logging companies.

When Lewis "Bert" Woodruff Chase moved to Walker with his family in 1894, he added his own layer of history. Bert was born on September 8, 1851, in New York; he married Louisa Hanson on January 2, 1887, in Wisconsin at Kilbourn City (now known as Wisconsin Dells). When he first arrived in Walker, it was a wild outpost on the edge of lawlessness, a male-dominated environment where tough uncompromising lumberjacks would roll in and out of the saloons that lined the streets. Bert had bought a plot of land with the dream of building a hotel and moved his wife and three children—Isabel, Edna, and Raymond Wallace—from Brainerd into a small tent he pitched on the site of his purchase. The family must have wondered what they had been brought to as they watched the antics of the locals from the scant protection of their temporary shelter, but they need not have worried, for what they were actually witnessing (as Bert broke the soil with his spade for the first time) was the creation of the Hotel Isabel—named after the couple's first daughter. Two more children, Loren and Natica, were later born in the relative comfort of the newly built hotel.

Walker was officially incorporated in 1896 following the arrival of the newly built railroad. The railroad industry

was booming and expanded further the following year, join-
ing Walker with Park Rapids and Cass Lake. This brought a
flood of new opportunities, and an influx of businesspeople
and travelers descended upon the town. This was the catalyst
for Bert to expand his own business by purchasing a second
hotel named the Pameda in 1897, which Bert renamed the
Chase Hotel (this site is now occupied by the village square).

A Tragic Family Death

By 1915 the rough nature of the town was starting to diminish and tourism started to boom; the railroad increased in
popularity and brought hundreds of fishermen and their
families north to experience the scenery of the third-largest
lake in Minnesota. The explosion of new visitors could not be
easily accommodated, however, and the town's infrastructure
failed to keep progress with the rise in its leisure industry. As
a result Walker became littered with tents dotted along the
shoreline as visitors were forced to camp out—just as Bert
and his family had done when they first arrived.

Bert had seen the necessity of providing accommodation and had the vision to turn this once small logging town
into a modern resort that could attract tourists from all over
America and beyond; feeling inspired, he started to build on
the site of the old Spencer Hotel. An architect named Johnson was brought in from Bemidji to design the new four-
story building; he created a state-of-the-art hotel with over
a hundred rooms, with suites equipped with their own bath,
toilet, and hot and cold running water. The dining room overlooked the lake and could accommodate over seventy-five
diners. Arthur "Archie" LaVigne was hired as the contractor

and employed a sash and door factory from St. Cloud, Sartell & Dunwold, which undertook the huge task of milling the doors and window.

The work started on October 11, 1918, when the first spade broke the soil to excavate the basement—reflecting what Bert had done twenty-four years previously. The first mortgage on the hotel was for $500 at an 8 percent rate of interest; this was through the First National Bank of Walker on March 1, 1922. It is believed the total cost for the project was $150,000—a staggering amount of money for 1922 and a reflection of Bert's business skills over the previous three decades. The opening of the hotel was not to be a joyous occasion, however, and what was to be a day of celebration turned into a day of mourning.

The Chases' son Loren had worked exhaustively on getting the new hotel built and finished on time; as the final touches were being implemented, he managed to catch a cold that quickly progressed to pneumonia. With his natural defenses low, due to the stress and tiredness of overworking, he succumbed to the illness, and died on May 27, 1922—just days before the grand opening. It was hoped that Loren would have run the new hotel and family business, allowing Bert to take a well-deserved retirement due to his own failing health. William Francis "Bill" Finnegan, Bert's son-in-law and Isabel's husband, had to step in instead to help ease the burden.

The hotel opened on June 8, 1922, but the event was overshadowed by Loren's death; the lobby was decorated with wreaths and not the flowers of a celebratory opening. The drapes were pulled, and the family attired themselves in traditional black—more akin to the graveside than the lakeside. It was from this somber stepping stone that the latest incarnation of the Chase Hotel opened its doors.

The historical significance of the hotel was finally recognized on June 4, 1980, when it was placed on the National Register of Historic Places—an event witnessed by an elderly Isabel Chase Finnegan, who died just five months later, on November 8, 1980.

INVESTIGATION

A Poltergeist in the Lobby

The lobby is part of the original building and managed to survive a devastating fire in 1997; it is the oldest part of the hotel and is believed to be the most haunted. The manager and several employees have experienced strange footsteps and shadow figures while working behind the reception desk.

Perhaps the most unusual incident involved the antique grandfather clock that stands on duty overlooking the proceedings. Its key is left in the lock on the front cover of the clock so that it does not become misplaced (as the clock is required to be wound on a regular basis). The employees have witnessed the key fly out of the clock and across the lobby on numerous occasions. During the reopening of the hotel in 2007, a display of the original black mourning dresses was placed in the lobby as an exhibit and memorial of when the hotel was first opened; the dresses were originally worn by members of Loren's family as a mark of respect. As the hotel was being reopened, a gust of wind blew through the lobby and visibly moved the swaying dresses; there were no rational

The original reception area and lobby, circa 1922

explanations for this phenomenon, as all the doors and windows in the lobby were closed.

This area promised to be the most active, so I organized a vigil in the cozy glow of the warm timber-paneled walls, sumptuous deep-red sofas, plush rugs, and antique hunting memorabilia. The ghost box had proven to be the most effective piece of equipment in the hotel, so I continued with what appeared to be working. I turned the device on and set up the recording equipment. Without any prompting, the ghost box shouted out, "Go!"

It is always disturbing when an entity directs an order at you with such vivacity. I am always respectful of the spirits I encounter, and I reassure them that I will leave shortly and that I just want to know their name and why they want me to leave. I asked for the name of the spirit that wanted me to go.

"Sarah," was the reply.

According to my records, there was no one named Sarah associated with the hotel, but my historical documentation did not list the names of everyday workers. It was also common in the past for people to be called by names other than their given name. I asked if they missed Loren. Hauntingly, the reply came in a long, drawn-out female wail:

"Loreeeeeen."

Several experienced, hardened paranormal investigators in the room drew a sharp, audible intake of breath.

"Is there somebody you miss here?" I continued.

"My son!" was the response in a sobbing cry.

I inquired if the entity was Loren's mother (according to my documentation her name was Isabel).

"In the name of…" was the response.

"In the name of what?" I inquired.

"In the name of Christ………ADRIAN!"

This was some of the most impressive ghost box evidence any of us had heard and witnessed. The entity was intelligently responding to my questioning by completing sentences and using my name without prompting. I have already mentioned that I am always very polite when engaging with those that have passed on, yet this spirit was becoming rude and aggressive, out of context to my questioning.

"Goddamn it!" it then shouted out.

Then the most bizarre set of circumstances presented itself. A second voice called out directly after the first voice (which had blasphemed) and said, "Language!"

A second entity had challenged the first entity by chastising it. I spent several minutes in stunned silence as I picked up the snippets of a conversation between two spirits—while I listened on.

"Dear friend."

"Why don't you show your face?"

"We must prepare."

"Go away."

"Help yourself."

It was difficult with only parts of the conversation audible to ascertain which bits were directed towards me and which parts was a dialogue between the two of them. I asked if there was somebody specific on the team they wanted to talk with, the reply came back:

"Steve, Stephen, Stephen."

Steve R. was standing to my right; I wanted to see if they personally knew Steve or whether they had just heard us saying his name during the course of the investigation. I asked if they knew how many children Steve had; it actually sang the reply in a melodic tone, "Two of them!"

Steve had two small children.

With that response, the room went quiet and the spirits appeared to leave, perhaps through a lack of energy or due to the indignation of feeling tested. No further contact was made in this location.

Death in Battle

Shadow figures are regularly glimpsed wandering through the corridors of the hotel by guests and employees. Footsteps are also heard behind individuals when there is no one there, and objects fly around of their own accord. I believe it requires a large amount of energy for an entity to be physical and move an object around or to have the weight to make an audible noise when walking. As previously discussed, I believe the negative energy of battle can be brought into a property; I wanted to explore this further and discovered through my research that the hotel was once used as temporary morgue for dead soldiers until they could be moved to a final resting place.

On October 5, 1898, the serene peace of Leech Lake was broken by a conflict that took place between the 3rd U.S. Infantry and the Pillager Chippewa Indians; this clash is referred to as the Battle of Sugar Point and became the last Indian uprising and confrontation between Native Americans and the U.S. Army.

The timber around Walker seemed to be at the center of most disagreements and arguments at this time. Thomas Walker himself had sold the ground on which the village was built to the Leech Lake Land Company, reserving all rights to the timber. He then sent in his own timber cutters, much to the consternation of the protesting local settlers. Their attempts to drive the cutters out of the local forests became the cause of bitter resentment for many years.

The loggers in Walker also harvested timber from the reservation, breaking previously agreed-upon annuity payments by withholding money or underestimating figures for the amount of timber taken. They also instigated a policy of setting fire to trees in order to pass them off as dead, as an agreement to harvest only dead timber was in place. The construction of dams in the vicinity also added to the disharmony, as this caused heavy flooding to the surrounding reservation, leaving many Indians displaced and homeless with their land rendered useless for hunting and cultivation.

Friction between the Pillagers and the local officials was heightened further by the mistreatment of tribal members who were arrested on overzealous and trivial offenses. The trials subsequently took place some distance from the Leech Lake reservation, in Duluth and Minneapolis; this left the accused (when acquitted) with a long and difficult journey home unaided.

The situation finally came to a head when a failed attempt was made to apprehend the Ojibwe chieftain Bugonaygeshig. He had started protesting against the unscrupulous practices of the logging companies, which brought him to the attention of the authorities. During a journey from a nearby Indian village to Onigum (another Indian settlement), he was apprehended and detained on the premise of being a witness to a bootlegging operation; this would have required him to be removed to Duluth to be present at a trial. As Bugonaygeshig was being led away, his captors came under attack from several disgruntled Pillagers and he managed to escape and evade recapture.

This incident led to a request from the local authorities for military assistance to help quell the mini-uprising and to facilitate the arrest of Bugonaygeshig. A response duly came from Fort Snelling in the shape of a twenty-strong regiment of infantry. This made little difference to the situation though, and scouts reported that Bugonaygeshig was still refusing to surrender. A larger reinforcement of seventy-seven men followed under the command of Brevet Major Melville C. Wilkinson and General John M. Bacon.

Before the soldiers engaged in conflict, they assembled at the shoreline of Leech Lake ready to be deployed. Louisa Chase cooked meals and provided coffee with a warm smile for the nervous men. They then sailed across the lake to a small peninsula on the northeast side via two steamships, the *Chief of Duluth* and the *Flora*. No one knows who fired the first shot—General Bacon believed that an accidental discharge of a soldier's rifle prompted the Pillagers to start firing at the regiment from the surrounding woods. The Pillagers later stated that the battle commenced after they witnessed several soldiers shooting at defenseless women in canoes as the steamships neared the peninsula.

A combination of inexperience and a lack of discipline amongst the soldiers resulted in early losses, and Wilkinson struggled to make any tactical advances. He himself was shot in the leg while trying to command his troops into better positions, and was forced to withdraw to the shelter of a log cabin that provided cover. Major Wilkinson returned to the heat of battle, with his leg now dressed, in an attempt to try and rally his troops, only to be shot for a second time in the abdomen. There was to be no return this time though, and Wilkinson died an hour later from his injuries.

Another officer lost his life when Sergeant William Butler was killed trying to reach General Bacon to inform him of the major's death. It is believed that the dead and wounded were then brought back to the hotel (Louisa would have witnessed the same soldiers she cared for being unloaded and laid to temporary rest in their makeshift morgue). In total, six soldiers lost their lives and ten others were wounded. An Indian policeman also lost his life during the skirmish, and five civilians were reported as injured. Bugonaygeshig was never recaptured.

The Spirit of Edward

This was the decadent decade of the Roaring Twenties for the wealthy; the resort's first guests arrived in extravagance via seaplanes, to be served five-course banquets before dancing the night away to the Charleston music of the Dot Van Orchestra of Bemidji. Cocktails could be sipped illegally in the moonlight while listening to the rhythmic sound of the water meeting the shore. In attendance that first night were the rich and influential citizens of Walker, including state senator Patrick McGarry (founder of Walker and a railway entrepreneur) and W. H. "Billy" Fawcett, founder of the Breezy Point resort and the popular magazine *Captain Billy's Whiz Bang.*

For those less wealthy, the basement was the place to be, where an underground speakeasy was in full flow. Patrons of a bygone age have been seen moving through this area in the direction of where the speakeasy was situated; the voices of folks having a good time and the buzz of a crowd drinking have been heard coming from this vicinity. The internal workings of the hotel's heating, electrics, and plumbing now expose themselves in this mechanical room, and tall people are required to bow their heads for fear of being struck.

I stood in the darkness with my equipment scattered around me, and I turned on the ghost box to see what contact could be made. I was hoping to access a patron from a bygone age. I listened for the first few minutes without engaging, as a series of incoherent noises and random words were thrown out into the space. Lisa then stepped forward and asked, "Can you say my name?"

The reply came through instantly.

"Lisa," it said in a male voice.

It is a common phenomenon that an entity can be aware of your name even if you have not introduced yourself. I then proceeded to introduce the members of the team by name, in the hope that I could encourage the entity to give me their name; I asked who was with us, and it clearly responded, "Edward."

"Hello, Edward," I said. I told him that my middle name was Edward.

"What year is it, Edward?" I asked.

"1905," was his reply. (In 1905 the site was home to the original Spencer Hotel and a lumberyard.)

"Did you used to work here?"

"Yes," he replied.

I did not expect to engage with a worker fifteen years or so before the speakeasy came into operation. I asked if there was anything he wanted me to do for him, and his answer came back instantaneously: "Feed the horses!"

A hotel at the beginning of the twentieth century in the Midwestern wilderness would certainly have to accommodate horses; it would have been the only way of accessing the area outside of the railroad. Hostlers would have been employed to oversee the stables that would have been erected next to the hotel; the lumberyard would have also used horses for transportation, heavy lifting, and pulling. It was possible that Edward was either an employee of the yard or a hotel stable worker. I knew that traditional horse feed or hay would have been difficult for us to access at short notice during this time of night, but I did recall seeing a bowl of fruit in the lobby.

"If I leave an apple, would that suffice, would that work?"

"Yes, an apple," Edward replied, followed by, "Thank you."

I said, "Thank you for talking with us," in return.

Edward appeared satisfied with the result of our conversation, because he then retreated—we had no further contact. I believe Edward's desire to fulfill his duty in caring for the horses had driven him to communicate with us from the other side.

At the end of the investigation we asked the hotel manager, who had witnessed the entire vigil, if he had an apple we could leave as a trigger object, as well as a glass of beer (for the entities that were frequenting the speakeasy). I placed the trigger objects on the table and drew around them onto a sheet of paper, so that if they moved in my absence I would be able to tell as much. I also took photographs to document their position and left the area. I was assured that no one would enter this location during the course of the night, and only the manager and one other member of staff had a key. I came back the following morning to find that the apple had moved (by a fraction of an inch) and the beer in the glass had receded by an inch.

CONCLUSION

One of the key issues of investigating the paranormal for me is the feeling that you can help spirits; you would have to be very hardhearted to turn away from an individual that asks you for help or expresses a sense of pain and loss. I always feel a sense of frustration, though, that I cannot always facilitate this with the tools I have available to me; certainly words of comfort and sympathy can be expressed, but this feels barely sufficient on most occasions.

Many investigators believe in the concept of being trapped between our world and the next, due to the spirit being unaware of what is required of them in going towards "the light." I also believe that some are unaware they are even dead. It is also possible that spirits are worried about being judged and continue to stay in a stasis between this world and the next, when they have led a morally poor life. Others may believe they have unfinished business or wish through a sense of duty to continue in the area they resided or worked in—they may feel they have a message to deliver or a task to perform before they can rest.

I hope that in some small way Edward feels able to move on, especially if he was concerned about the welfare of his animals—further investigations should indicate if he is still around or not. Christian thinking would argue that if God has chosen not to embrace an individual after ending their life by not showing them the path they need to take, then who are we to encourage spirits in this process (as this goes against the will of God)? I do know that I find it hard not to help when it is asked for, especially as I am the one who has initiated the contact on most occasions. If something as simple as leaving an apple helps an individual gain some peace, then I will stand by that decision.

I hoped that contact would be made with Bert or the other members of his family during this investigation—but this was not forthcoming. Bert died in the hotel on July 17,

1938, after a seven-year battle with throat cancer. Just six years later Bill Finnegan died of a heart attack while participating in a duck hunt on September 20, 1944. Isabel and her mother, Louisa, continued to operate the hotel for another four years before finally selling up, thus ending a dynasty and an era. I also wanted to engage with the soldiers or the libation-fueled crowds that thronged the speakeasy—but in the end I was happy to settle for a well-mannered and dedicated hostler from 1905.

I came back with my team to the Chase resort recently; one of the most significant aspects of this follow-up investigation was the way in which the spirits conducted themselves in such a fervently aggressive manner. Steve R. took a team into the previously uninvestigated laundry room, and on two separate occasions proceeded to record a whole string of EVPs that shouted out, "Go, go, leave, get out, go!" Interestingly, the whole team picked up these EVPs on multiple devices—it would appear that the spirits are less welcoming of my team than the helpful and accommodating Chase resort staff.

CHAPTER 7

S.S. William A. Irvin

DULUTH

Strange ghostly noises, the horrific death of a sailor, and the sighting of a phantom pair of legs would suggest that "worse things do happen at sea!"

I took the team to Duluth on a bitterly cold, miserable January day for a single investigation (the weather became so bad that Steve R. actually crashed his car on the way to the location). I had wanted to investigate the S.S. *William A. Irvin* for some time, and the owners very kindly agreed to accommodate us. A substantial amount of detail and research was obtained from our guide who showed us around the vessel. She was very knowledgeable about its history and brought with her copies of newspaper reports relating to relevant incidents—their website was also a useful tool as a starting point. Period newspapers accessed at the Duluth Historical

Society expanded my research, and books detailing ghostly encounters on Lake Superior were prolific.

HISTORY

The S.S. *William A. Irvin* is a towering reddish-brown wall of sheet metal whose mass sits serenely in the dock next to the Aerial Lift Bridge in Duluth; her night-lit moorings highlight her elegance and illuminate the bulk freighter's 610-foot length. This calm retiring place belies her forty years of industrial service as a maritime workhorse plowing a determined furrow through some of the most dangerous waters in the world. The *Irvin* traversed the Great Lakes as part of the Pittsburgh Steamship Division of the U.S. Steel's fleet; she was built by the American Ship Building Company in Lorain, Ohio, at a cost of $1.3 million—a considerable sum of money during the Great Depression. She was launched on November 10, 1937, and embarked on her maiden voyage on June 25, 1938. She then underwent sea trials before beginning her role of transporting bulk materials from the tip of Lake Superior's Two Harbors to the steel mills of Lake Michigan and Lake Erie.

The *Irvin* has a beam (width) of sixty feet and a depth of more than thirty-two feet; her carrying capacity was 14,000 gross tons. She was used to transport iron ore and taconite straight from the mines, but also carried coal and limestone throughout her career—she was fitted to carry grain but never fulfilled this duty due to the complications attached to switching cargo types. Her classification as a *Straight Decker* is down to the forward pilot house (to meet the navigational demands of the lakes) with the engines aft (towards the stern).

The S. S. William A. Irvin

INVESTIGATION

The Cargo Hold

The *Irvin* was the first freight ship to have all its internal areas accessible from the inside; this allowed the crew to stay below the deck in subzero temperatures. Within this maze of metallic, cold corridors many mysterious sightings have taken place, and the slamming of industrial steel doors appear to be caused by more than a stiff Lake Superior wind. The flickering lights could be attributed to the archaic worn wiring, but in the stillness and sanctuary of the sealed dock, any abnormal electrical occurrences should be investigated as possible paranormal activity. Blackouts were common when the *Irvin* was a working ship; the onboard sound-powered telephones were then used to communicate in the darkness. We would be using our two-way radios.

The first vigil was to commence in the depths of the cargo hold. I felt a sense of apprehension as I started my descent—probably caused by the messages my brain was receiving about how forebodingly black and monumentally cavernous the space was. The noise of the team following me down the metal stairs sounded like a wrench being violently shaken in a large, empty can, as the hollow ship emphasized the introduction of human activity. If spirits were residing down here, I would not be taking them by surprise. I took an initial baseline temperature reading of −7 degrees Fahrenheit, but I did not need a thermometer to inform me of the impending discomfort of the vigil; the sight of my breath billowing and dissipating into the frigid, damp, dark air provided that indication (I was below the waterline in an expansive metal box surrounded by a frozen lake). The sound of the ice cracking and maneuvering against the metal hull was deafening at times—these odd, jarringly uncomfortable noises may have been falsely attributed to paranormal activity in the past.

As I walked the 600 feet to the farthest part of the hold, I began to note that the discussions I shared with the team were becoming noticeably indistinguishable, as the words they said merged together in a bouncing assault of echoing noise that left the sentences blurred and unintelligible. This phenomenon would render my recorded evidence redundant.

The cargo hold is divided into three sections. I set up my equipment in the aft (back) section of the ship. Stored in this location are the items for the haunted tour the ship provides in October, along with tools and a forklift. It was certainly a new experience to be conducting a vigil surrounded by a collection of creepy dolls, brutally severed limbs, and a blood-splattered mannequin that appeared to be in the throes of a disemboweling.

I started by using the ghost box, to see if any entities wished to discover who was creating the noise and making the disturbance. I explained to those willing to listen how the equipment worked and the differing ways they could communicate with me. Shortly into the vigil, a sound—like somebody walking on the deck above—was clearly heard, followed by the noise of a door slamming in the main section of the hold. Team member Steve R. went to investigate and found nobody present. These sounds would be difficult to present as paranormal evidence though, due to the many other noises that were taking place around me.

My audio evidence was contaminated; my trigger objects failed to move; the ghost box remained unusually quiet; and my fingers were blue. I did wonder why an entity would consider frequenting a disused hold on a cargo freighter—this was backed up by my impressive lack of evidence. I hoped the investigation would pick up in the more habitable parts of the ship.

As I walked back through the sections, I decided to explore the area between the inner and outer hull, but at that very moment I engaged in an internal dialogue that reviewed the merits of venturing too far—as my flashlight appeared to be fading fast. The thought of being trapped on my own, deep between the sloping narrow space of the watery outer and inner hulls (without the aid of a flashlight), edged me outside of my comfort zone. Luckily the left-hand side of my brain prevailed, with its years of investigative experience and reasoning ability, overpowering the right side with its reckless youthful enthusiasm—because ten minutes later my flashlight flickered and died.

Ghost Ships

All the cargo on the *Irvin* was loaded and unloaded through eighteen hatches via the deck; each section of the hold was covered in a giant, one-piece, solid 5.5-ton hatch cover that would be removed using the hatch crane. The hatch covers would be replaced after use and securely clamped down using butterfly or dog-ear clamps. This was a vital and integral safety precaution, as the powerful lake storms and waves could easily wash over the deck and flip open a hatch despite their weight. The importance placed upon this process was highlighted on November 10, 1975, when the S.S. *Edmund Fitzgerald* (one of the largest lake freighters) sank suddenly in Lake Superior—just seventeen miles from the entrance of Whitefish Bay (she went down with such speed that she was unable to send a distress signal). The entire crew of twenty perished and no bodies were recovered.

An investigation led by the Coast Guard suggested that the hatches had not been effectively closed and water had breached the hold due to severe storm conditions, rendering the ship unstable over time. The ship sank quickly due to its lack of buoyancy and broke apart upon impact with the lake bed at a depth of 530 feet. Ten years after the disaster a commercial vessel claimed to have identified the *Fitzgerald* sailing in the misty distance; this sighting adds to the growing list of ghost ships that are said to traverse the lake. A ghost ship is an apparition caused by the residual haunting of a vessel that has been lost at sea but is still occasionally observed sailing.

It is believed the total number of shipping losses on the Great Lakes over a 300-year period is close to 25,000—with 6,000 of those taking place within a twenty-year period between 1878 and 1897 (with the loss of 1,166 lives). It is then no surprise that fervent ghost stories and tales of watery hauntings are recounted, in horror and in abundance, by those who have spent their lives working on the Great Lakes—a fact that was noted by the *Minneapolis Journal* on July 20, 1901:

Landsmen boast of their haunted houses and the weird spirits that dance in country graveyards at midnight. But there's not a house, no matter how black and dismal and how far back from the road it may be sitting, nor how many murders may have been committed within its walls years ago, that can compare in supernatural terrors with the haunted ships with their crews of dead men that haunt their trackless waves of the water.[30]

The oldest vessel recorded as a ghost ship is the sighting of the *Le Griffon*, which vanished in 1678; numerous sailors over the centuries since then have reported seeing her phantom hulk silently drifting into view, through the chilling swirling mists of a winter's night. Perhaps the most terrifying encounter with an aqueous apparition came when a recreational diver explored the wreck of the *Emperor* in 1988. The *Emperor* was a 1910 steel-ore steamer—similar to the *Irvin*; she sank on June 4, 1947, on the rocks at Isle Royale, with the loss of twelve crewmen.

The diver ventured inside the wreck to explore the cabin quarters—where he saw a crewman reclined on a bunk. The ghost turned to look at the underwater explorer, fixing him with a blank expression. The diver removed himself from the wreck as quickly as his flippers could take him.

This kind of maritime ghostly encounter appears to be more chilling and fear-inducing than any land-based entity could entertain. That may be due to the unique way in which a ship can quickly become a tomb, embracing the sailors in a perfectly preserved state after the trauma of drowning. As the *Minneapolis Journal* put it in 1901:

> There's not a ghost on land, no matter how many graveyards he may prowl around, nor how many old mansions he may rattle chains in and groan and disport himself, that can hold his head up for one minute

in the presence of one of the gristly, grinning, matted, dark ghosts on a ghost ship.[31]

A second ghostly figure has also been seen in the engine room of the *Emperor* that made similar eye contact with a diver. This apparition was seen proceeding with the duties of checking and operating the engine—the common phenomenon of observing a worker fulfilling his obligations after his death, like Edward at the Chase resort. The residual haunting drone of the engines has also been heard through the deathly cold entombing water—despite the obvious fact they would be inoperable.

It is worth noting that during the mid-1970s a sailor's body was found trapped face-down in the engine room and was subsequently recovered. Legend claims that "Lake Superior seldom gives up her dead," and this was certainly true for the crew of the ill-fated S.S. *Edmund Fitzgerald* and the *Emperor*—until the single discovery of the unfortunate engine-room body. But this legend can be explained with scientific fact; the bacterium that multiplies inside a sunken corpse produces gases that eventually cause the body to rise to the surface. The low yearly average water temperature of Lake Superior is enough to suppress the spread and growth of bacteria, thus keeping the bodies firmly at the bottom.

The Phantom Legs

The crew dining area of the *Irvin* can be accessed from outside via the back of the ship. The floor was treacherously slippery, and I practically clawed my way around the walls to get to the galley. This added to the ever-growing myriad of possible concussions, contusions, sprains, scrapes, breaks, and discomforts the ship was storing up for any unwitting investigator. The galley was swathed in a sea of clinically clean brushed-steel surfaces; old food packets containing oats, salt, rice, and other comestibles sat in faded 1970s packaging on the shiny shelving. Everything I touched inside the ship was cold—the doors, handrails, fixtures, and fittings (even the walls are painted in shades of gray, blue, and aquamarine).

The crew's quarters had all the welcoming appeal of a prison cell, and were furnished less well, so I progressed to the more luxurious guests' quarters at the front of the ship. The *Irvin* was unusual in having a three-tiered bow cabin; most lake freighters were built with only two levels. This extra deck was put to good use as luxury accommodation for guests of the steel company; there was a suite of four cabins and a guest lounge with a dining room located where most freighters would house their second hatch.

The guest lounge was gloomy, as the windows were boarded up for the winter; it was trimmed in oak paneling, walnut veneer, and brass. For a brief moment it transported me to the cruiseliner world of fine dining and comfort. Steve R. left the room briefly to set down an equipment case at the base of the stairs; I scoured the environment with my camera. Two black-and-white portraits of William and Gertrude Irvin stared back at me through the camera lens that I pointed towards the far wall. The ship was named after William Irvin, the fourth president of the U.S. Steel corporation. Irvin dropped out of school and went straight into the mines, where he managed to work his way up to the position of president. Irvin and his second wife, Gertrude, were the very first guests to be invited onboard the ship.

Steve R. then sprang back into the room to tell me he had seen an apparition on the stairs; we rushed back outside and looked up at the dimly lit steps. He said he turned towards the stairs from a crouching position and saw what appeared to be a pair of legs descending towards him; they were only visible from the knee down. We quickly ran our equipment over the area but recorded no significant results. We re-created Steve's movements to see if some sort of reflection or trick of the light had taken place—but this was not the case. I thought perhaps another team member may have been outside on the main deck and created an illusion in some way with a stray flashlight, but Steve and I were the only two people at that end of the ship. As the vigil had not yet started (we were just gathering data), no equipment was running to back up this experience. However, later, in the lounge, I received a response in regard to the incident, when I asked the ghost box if Steve R. had seen someone on the stairs—the reply was "Yes."

The sight of a pair of ghostly legs descending the stairs leaves many unanswered questions—such as, what happened to the rest of the body? There are many examples throughout paranormal history of ghosts that are not fully formed or have body parts missing. Ghosts in Japanese culture are traditionally represented without legs, normally depicted drifting on a cloud of smoke. Phantom floating heads are often seen, and are a phenomenon of the St. James Hotel in Red Wing. A particularly famous haunting in York, England, was of a Roman army marching through a cellar—they were only visible from the knees up (as the Roman road they were matching on was a foot below the current floor level). I considered that the layout of the ship's interior may have caused such an unusual vision, if the floors or corridors inside the pilot house had been moved around, but this would be unlikely, as a very large can opener indeed would be required to alter the internal schematic of the ship.

I wondered if an industrial accident may have resulted in the severing of legs, but I could find no record of such an event to back up this theory. It could also be suggested that the manifestation was actually full, but Steve R. only had the ability to see a limited amount of the entity at that time (sometimes it is the viewer and not what is being viewed that makes the distortion). Steve R. spent the rest of the evening, like many other paranormal investigators, questioning what he saw; sometimes when a normal explanation for an event cannot found, we need to look above and beyond the norm—this is what we then call paranormal. Sometimes our brain wants to talk us out of our experience because it goes against what science tells us is possible and what we are told to believe. On many occasions I have pondered on the experiences I have encountered and tried to find ways to dismiss them or explain them away; a healthy skepticism is a vital character trait in any investigator, but sometimes you just have to acknowledge that some incidents are beyond comprehension.

A Tragic, Horrifying Death

The engine room is a reverential celebration of the steam era, complete with gleaming brass, pristine marine-gray paintwork, and more dials, levers, buttons, and valves than seem remotely necessary. The whole three-story auditorium of 1930s cutting-edge, coal-driven steam equipment appears remarkably clean and airy. The Irvin was fitted with a geared De Laval cross-compound steam turbine engine, which was unusual during this period of construction, as most ore freighters were powered by the towering reciprocating triple-expansion steam engine.

The Irvin needed to carry up to 266 tons of coal, which it stored above the boiler room and delivered via the gravity-fed coal burner—it burned up to 1.2 tons of coal per hour to generate the steam. The steam powered the turbine under high pressure, generating 5,600 rpm, before reduction gears slowed the propeller shaft to a manageable 90 rpm. A second low-pressure turbine made use of the waste steam to give the Irvin a combined fully loaded speed of 11.1 mph (12.5 mph when empty), with over 2,000 horsepower. This actually made the Irvin one of the slowest ships in the fleet, but its longevity was achieved through its cost-effectiveness (due to the low coal consumption)—faster ships could reach speeds of 20 mph but were duly scrapped due to their poor economy.

The boiler room (adjacent to the engine room) became the scene of a horrific death in 1964, when the Irvin was en route to Duluth with her iron-ore cargo for the first trip of the year after her winter mooring. William Wuori, an experienced fifty-nine-year-old crew member from International Falls, was on watch in the fire room with two work colleagues. Suddenly a boiler tube ruptured, spraying water onto the boiler fire, which exploded into a violent burst of scalding steam that stripped the men of their skin. Wuori died an agonizing death—the two other men were hospitalized with serious injuries but survived.

The engine room and adjoining boiler room were recorded at a more comfortable 12 degrees Fahrenheit as we started the second vigil. I decided against asking the spirits for a sign of their presence as the ice could still be heard shifting around outside; this noise was now joined by a distant hum that emanated from the old electrical paneling, providing a constant bass note to the whole symphony. I placed several EMF meters in strategic places on the walkways and doors, where regular traffic would have flowed—in the hope of recording a residual haunting. I then turned on the Ovilus and began to make notes, as Lou called out into the echoing space in the hope of engaging with a spirit. The device replied, "Lady."

"I don't suppose you had many women in here," replied Lou.

"Goodbye," was the retort.

"Do you want us to leave?" she continued, but no further response was forthcoming.

It was generally considered bad luck to have a woman onboard a ship; ancient superstition is deeply ingrained in the history of seafaring over the centuries, although these myths and ideas have long since been forgotten. An example from the year 1379 illustrates how seriously mariners took this particular omen. During an unusually violent storm off the coast of Cornwall, England, sailors gave in to their irrational fear with harrowing consequences when they started to throw panic-stricken women (many of them nuns) off the ship and into a watery grave. Over sixty women drowned that fateful night due to the sailors' misguided and superstitious hope of appeasing the storm. The majority of the men also perished—including the commanding officer, Baron John Arundel of Lanherne.

The Ovilus continued to present a string of words that were remarkably relevant to the area we were investigating:

"Heat—hurt—scream—travel—cry."

Unfortunately, I could not instigate a response to any of the questions I asked; these five words came in isolation without any prompting. I felt a frustrating sense of being watched but found it difficult to promote a full interaction. It would be true to say that the more times you investigate a site, the more frequent the contact becomes, as if those entities residing there are getting used to you and are beginning to show a level of trust.

CONCLUSION

From a historic point of view, industrial heritage is not given the same prestige and focus as other projects—the Great Lakes' Hulett cranes would be an example of that trend. The Hulett crane was an integral part of the shipping process on the lakes; they made redundant the raw manual labor required to empty the freighters by hand using just buckets and hoists. This method was time-consuming and took several days to complete; the Hulett took only five to ten hours to clear a freighter and reduced the cost of doing so considerably. On August 27, 1940, the *Irvin* set a record for quickest unloading time: the Hulett cranes emptied the hold of 13,856 tons of ore in two hours and fifty-five minutes. This feat will never be broken, as modern ships use automatic self-unloaders in the bottom of their cargo holds.

The Huletts were very much part of the Great Lakes' dockside landscape but were rarely used outside of this environment. (Huletts could not adjust themselves to the ebb and flow of salt-water tides when in operation.) The Huletts were finally decommissioned in 1992, and there are now only six left in existence. This is part of the Great Lakes' industrial heritage that appears to be held in scant regard—despite being placed on the National Register of Historic Places and designated as a Historic Mechanical Engineering Landmark. The last Huletts in Cleveland were recently demolished as part of a redevelopment plan.

The Irvin was in service from 1938 until 1975; she was then used as a general workhorse until her retirement in 1978. The Irvin sat in layup in West Duluth for eight years until a nonprofit organization purchased her for $110,000, as an addition to their waterfront convention center.

Even though the Irvin was sitting tranquilly in the dock during this investigation, it was the most testing of environments I have ever tried to obtain evidence from—it could well be categorized as an outside investigation but for a thin layer of sheet metal; it was an assault on the senses from the first moment I placed a foot on the noisy deck. The bombardment of sounds kept me edgy and unfocused; the lack of vision and the cold in the cargo hold distracted me and blunted my senses—then drained my power supplies. Thankfully, I will never have to work on a bulk freighter in high waters, but I got an insight into how harsh and dangerous making a living on the lakes of Minnesota could be during the last century.

CHAPTER 8

The Opera House

MANTORVILLE

The phantom of a dead actress, a ghost cat, and a haunted piano all make a night at the opera a very chilling experience.

I have investigated three times at the Opera House in Mantorville, Dodge County. The owners of the property have always been very friendly and accommodating to my team. The entire town has embraced this attitude as well, as they are proud of their heritage and look to promote their historical past fully. The Dodge County Historical Society in Mantorville was very helpful in allowing me to access their documents, and our guides at the theater also provided valuable information—which was backed up by period newspaper articles and online research.

HISTORY

Mantorville is located along the south branch of the middle fork of the Zumbro River, eighteen miles to the west of Rochester. Early pioneers made their way farther west of the Mississippi, expanding outwards from La Crosse and other riverside settlements, into the uncharted land of the Great Plains—among these were Frank Mantor and John Hubbell. They were traveling on a stagecoach in 1853, from Winona to St. Peter, when they jumped off and staked a claim to the land they were standing on. Frank was quickly joined by his brothers Peter and Riley, and they gave their name to the new settlement. The Mantor brothers were born in Albany County, New York, but moved at a young age when the family purchased land to start a farm in Linesville, Crawford County, Pennsylvania. As the boys grew older, they showed their level of ambition by traveling west to find suitable land to start their own businesses.

The Mantor brothers could see the benefits of using the natural resources available to them—these included the limestone, the seemingly never-ending tracts of hilly woodland, and the river. Frank and John went straight to work and opened a general store and grist mill; the timber they processed was used for the construction of the town's buildings. This infrastructure allowed the population to rise rapidly in 1854 to 100 (the year the town was officially recognized); a further 400 settlers arrived over the next three years, adding to the town's expansion. By 1860 the population had increased to 760.

One of the determining factors in Mantorville's quick success was the abundance of local limestone; quarries provided a regular source of employment and supplied the raw materials needed to develop the town. Limestone is soft and easily carved when first extracted; it then becomes harder when it is exposed to the elements—making it the perfect long-lasting building material. Mantorville limestone was used all over Minnesota, including in the St. Mary's Hospital building in Rochester and the Dodge County courthouse in Mantorville (the oldest working courthouse in Minnesota). The courthouse was started in 1865 at a cost of $15,000; the forty-inch-thick monolithic blocks of limestone were slid over frozen ground to the building site.

John Hubbell constructed Mantorville's first hotel in 1854 by utilizing the rich resource of local timber; its double roof design allowed for extra guest rooms. A larger, more permanent structure was required after just two years due to the demand for rooms; a three-story stone building was then constructed. Its popularity steadily increased as the Hubbell House became a well-known refuge for travelers making their way from the Mississippi River to the St. Peter trail. Stone threshold steps lead to the entrance on the southwest corner and show the evidence of every guest who has been fortunate enough to enter, as the steps dip in the middle through wear.

On long, hot summer evenings, stagecoach drivers, mail couriers, and travelers would sit outside and smoke, telling tales of daring. The guest book documents the rich and varied history of the prominent travelers who have stayed there: Senator Alexander Ramsey, the second governor of Minnesota and later U.S. Secretary of War under President Rutherford B. Hayes; General Ulysses S. Grant, later the eighteenth President of the United States; Ole Bornemann Bull, Norwegian violinist and composer; Horace Greeley, member of the U.S. House of Representatives, *New York Tribune* editor, and a founder of the Liberal Republican Party; William W. Mayo, doctor, chemist, and founder of the Mayo Clinic; and the Rt. Rev. Henry B. Whipple, the first Episcopal bishop of Minnesota.

John Hubbell did not build upon the burgeoning success of his business though, as he mysteriously went missing. It was maliciously rumored that he may have owed money from gambling debts, but he was never seen again in Mantorville and his disappearance has been the source of local gossip. I hoped that during the course of the investigation I would get the opportunity to ask a spirit about this strange event and that it might be possible to talk with John Hubbell himself.

HISTORY OF THE OPERA HOUSE

The Mantorville Opera House was constructed in 1918 on the smoldering site of a general store that burned down as part of a row of businesses. The Opera House entertained the local townsfolk and became their only distraction outside of the insalubrious saloons that decorated the town's streets. A transient audience was also appreciative of the shows, and many stopped there to break up their journey while passing through the prairies of southeastern Minnesota—some were entertainers themselves looking for employment that evening. Traveling vaudeville acts visited the town; this was a popular form of entertainment in the early part of the twentieth century. The folks of Mantorville generated a buzz of anticipation, as neighbors and friends met to discuss local news before the hush induced by a parting curtain. Regular patrons would have been witness to the slow evolution of theater entertainment.

It would have been common for singers and novelty acts to perform between the breaks of a standard play; this became the genesis of vaudeville (which placed a string of unrelated acts on the same bill). This would include comedy routines, musicians, impersonators, acrobats, jugglers, thinly dressed dancing girls, and lecturing celebrities. This approach was then slowly replaced by musical theater, which tried to integrate many of the acts into a single play. *Show Boat,* based on the 1926 novel by Midwestern author Edna Ferber, would have been one of the first musical shows to play, embracing the idea of having nonmusical scenes introduced to the story to enrich the narrative. This idea developed further with the show *Oklahoma!* by Rodgers and Hammerstein; this musical integrated dream ballet scenes to help carry the plot and develop the characters.

The Opera House served many purposes throughout its history—as one would expect of a large building in a small town. In the late 1920s, after a decline in the popularity of live entertainment, it joined the saloons and embraced the sale and celebration of alcoholic consumption—becoming a speakeasy and later a drinking club. Massive social changes also affected the type of productions that were shown to the dwindling audiences. Plays took on the themes of social roles and tried to identify more with the unemployed and the plight of the immigrant. Government subsides supplied by the Federal Theatre Project (whose goal was to create

The Mantorville Opera House, built in 1918

employment for performers, writers, directors, and artists) helped to provide funding for poorer audiences to see controversial and thought-provoking plays—such as the stage adaptation of the novel *It Can't Happen Here*, by Minnesota native Sinclair Lewis.

The wealthier members of the audience also started to stay at home with the introduction of home entertainment, which included cheaper and more accessible books and publications, radios, gramophones, and eventually television. Ironically, the earliest radio and television productions were influenced heavily by vaudeville entertainment—as they drew from the same pool of talent, creating employment opportunities for those performers who had lost their theater jobs.

The Opera House also served the community as a municipal town hall, a civic center, and even a roller rink in the 1950s, before being re-embraced by the Mantorville Theatre Company in the 1970s. Once again the townsfolk would tread the stage boards, echoing what their forefathers had done—when the wood was still sticky from its first coat of varnish. As the building became frequented again, the patrons and employees began to witness and experience paranormal phenomena: the sound of a ghostly footstep accompanied by a descending dark mist, the sensation of cold spots, and the phantom throw of a light switch.

THEATER GHOSTS AND SUPERSTITIONS

I was told by local residents and historians, Jane Olive and Melisa Ferris, that other investigators had difficulty in successfully contacting the resident ghosts and spirits. When they asked if anyone was willing to talk with them, they received several responses of "Shut up!"

This of course is a riposte that acts like a full stop when trying to facilitate a dialogue. I did consider that this may be the response made to anyone making a noise during a theater production—there may have been a ghostly play taking place during their investigation. Ghosts and theaters have always shared a history of superstition; it is believed theaters should close for one night a week to provide an opportunity for ghosts to perform their own plays—perhaps that was their night. Traditionally this is a Monday, which conveniently gives the actors and backstage crew a night off after their weekend performances.

It is also a common superstitious belief that a light should always be left on in an empty theater; the light would be placed at the front center of the stage, close to where the audience would be—this was to provide an opportunity for ghosts to read their scripts. Failure to provide the light was believed to make ghosts angry and would lead to pranks and mischief. This folklore probably has its roots in ancient health and safety procedures; a continually illuminated stage would help to ensure the theater staff did not fall over the set or drop into the orchestra pit. The cluttered backstage area could be a hazardous place for anyone stumbling around in the dark looking for a light switch.

INVESTIGATION

The Phantom Actress

I started the first vigil in the basement. It was a common practice for dressing rooms to be located under the theater during this period; performers had to practice their lines, change costumes, and apply their makeup in the damp confines of this gloomy environment.

One actress was going through this routine when she became distracted by the appearance of a lady wearing a near-identical dress to her own; the friendly intruder spoke to the actress about the same role she had played many years previously. The actress turned briefly to place her script on the dressing table and turned back to find the lady gone. The startled actress fled up the stairs, two steps at a time, and bounded into the arms of a colleague; in a frightened state she breathily started to tell of her ghostly encounter. She only got as far as her opening sentence, though, before letting out an audible gasp; she could now see the shadowy, strange woman appearing high up in the balcony area, still wearing the costume they shared. Both actors witnessed the phantom actress weaving around the lofty heights of the auditorium; they hastily gathered their personal belongings and left with the rest of the cast, never to return. Patrons received a refund on their tickets for that night's performance.

Jane and Melisa told me that the ghostly actress is widely known to the local citizenry; her name is Ellen and she roams the corridors and aisles—often ascending the stairs to where the women's dressing room is now located. Her name was revealed by a group of college students messing around with a Ouija board in the 1970s when they should have been rehearsing. Whether her name is correct or not remains to be seen, but sometimes just the act of acknowledgment can be the basis for contact. Ellen now gets the blame whenever props, keys, jewelry, and other items go missing backstage.

These items always turn up eventually, usually somewhere where they weren't left—like the costume glasses left on a table before a play that turned up again in a apron pocket worn by an actress just seconds before she went onstage.

Ellen also has the habit of playing with the theater's electrics; this frustrates the technicians greatly, as their lighting and sound can go awry during a performance. Whether she does this through a sense of playfulness or as a darker malevolent way of trying to stop or disrupt the show is unclear. Her attraction to the Opera House and dressing room, in connection with her participation in the productions and dialogue with the startled actress, would suggest she was a performer. The smell of heavy perfume left in the air would also indicate that she is dressed to entertain—it would be easy to imagine her in stage makeup, clothed resplendently and adorned in glittering costume jewelry.

The limited historical records provide no evidence of an actress dying during a performance or in the building, but a traveling troupe may have played at the Opera House during its illustrious history, and a deceased actress may be coming back to the venue she loved—to continue to share the stage with the living.

The Ghost Cat

The basement appeared devoid of the customary cobwebs and ingrained layers of grime that normally accompany my subterranean vigils, although a recent flood may have swept that aside in a dismissive, watery wave. Evidence of clandestine criminality littered the many hidden nooks of the basement with period bottles; it pointed to a history of illegal, surreptitious alcohol consumption—the dangers of leaving the evidence of empty bottles on public display had obviously been considered.

In one of the darker recesses, towards the far corner, was a hole that had been excavated. Barely big enough to wriggle through, it revealed a thin layer of crawlspace that allowed access to the underside of the stage. I saw a petrified cat in this area—its dusty, emaciated, angular form was still perfectly intact, like an Egyptian antiquity.

The only recorded death surrounding the Opera House took place during the production of a school play and adds to the theme of unlucky felines. Four schoolgirls discovered a black cat in the building. They petted the animal and picked it up; the cat was then startled by an unseen presence and leapt from a student's arms and out into the road—where it was fatally hit by a passing car. That night Ellen was particularly active: the building's electrics were again in a state of disarray; doors slammed; and cold spots were felt throughout the auditorium. Was it possible that Ellen was active in reflection of her unhappiness at spooking the cat, or was she expressing the happiness of having a cat to entertain her on the other side?

I began the vigil by turning on the ghost box; it instantly spat out the word *Ashley*, in a fervently female voice, followed by *Steve*, in a male voice. It then said, "Ashley" again and followed that directly with "Ash."

Both Ashley and Steve R. were working in a separate vigil in the upstairs dressing rooms and auditorium. It sounded like somebody was trying to get their attention, and I had inadvertently come in halfway through the conversation. I made a note of the time and would ask them after the vigil what they were doing at that very moment to see what could have elicited such a response.

The room then became significantly colder. I took a series of temperature readings to note the change in conditions, but found to my surprise the readings had not changed from the baseline temperature readings—yet the whole investigation team agreed it felt colder. I told the team how cold I had become, and the ghost box interceded by saying, "Yes, it's freezing."

"Are you making it cold?" I inquired.

"Me?" it replied in quizzical manner.

"How many of you are there?" I asked.

"Nine," it replied.

"So are there are nine people with us?"

"Nine," it replied once more, to verify the question.

"So how many would like to speak with me?"

"Eight," was then said. So, one spirit did not want to talk—or was it the cat?

At the beginning of the vigil I placed two K2 EMF meters in the room, one on the floor in front of me and a second in the narrow entrance that leads below the stage. Throughout the first twenty minutes of the vigil the meters registered a neutral reading of below 1.5 milligauss. As we progressed with our contact, via the ghost box, the meters both jumped to a constant reading of 10 milligauss and stayed there without fluctuating for a further twenty-five minutes.

I have never seen such a constant, uninterrupted reading like this without outside, nonparanormal electrical interference. The K2 has a limited range of around five inches, so to see two devices react in the same way, at the same time, in different parts of the basement, would suggest an omnipresent force that envelopes the space.

I then noticed what sounded like the noise of a cat purring and a meowing, coming through on the ghost box. I did not want to acknowledge this at first, as I thought this would be too fanciful to believe. I thought I must have given myself the suggestion of a cat presence, so I tried to convince myself that I had misheard this in amongst the white noise. I should perhaps have more faith in my abilities though, as feline noises were clearly heard during the evidence review of the audio recordings.

Due to the increased EMF activity and the progressively darker atmosphere (which fell like a giant paranormal cape), I asked if we were welcome. The ghost box replied, "Go!"

I waited for another response and received the word Go a further two times. The vigil was coming to an end, and I did not have the intention of being disrespectful, so we left. This decision was coupled with a sense of foreboding the team had felt that filled us with a claustrophobic oppression that became uncomfortable to withstand.

I made my way back to the control area and met up with Steve R. and Ashley; I told Steve about his name being called out, and I asked him to go back through his notes to find out what he was doing at that precise moment. He said that he went to explore the dressing room on the top floor after hearing a loud groan coming from the area. It could be suggested that an entity had called out for Steve R. and Ashley to gain their attention as they were looking, and I had then inadvertently picked up the words in a separate part of the building.

Steve R. and Ashley may have been looking straight through a spirit at that time without even realizing it. Remarkably, Steve R. said he asked shortly afterwards how many spirits wanted to communicate with him and received the exact same response I had received in the basement: "Eight."

Spirits of the Mantor Brothers

I started the second vigil on the stage facing out into the auditorium; this gave me a direct view of the balcony—the sight of shadow figures is a regular occurrence in this location. When the entities realize they have been seen, they duck down below the railings to hide their presence—this would suggest an intelligent haunting. The figures are dense in their appearance and can block out the detail of the wall and background behind them as they pass.

Team member Heather commented on the strong fragrance of almonds that suddenly became noticeable in the air; this is a phenomenon that is associated with Ellen, who creates the slight breath of a breeze on your skin as she makes her way by and leaves the traces of her perfume hanging distinctively in the air as further proof of her passing. I turned on the ghost box after our success with it in the basement and asked who was with us.

"Frank," was the response. I sat quietly pondering my next question when it said, "Frank," for a second time.

"I hear you, Frank. Thank you," I replied.

"Do you have anyone with you?" I inquired.

"Peter," was the response.

"Do you prefer Peter or Pete?" I asked.

"Pete," it answered, as the K2 EMF meter spiked in time with the response to register a higher reading.

The names Frank and Peter are the same as the Mantor brothers who originally founded Mantorville; this seemed like an incredible coincidence, so I ventured to ask if they knew what happened to John Hubbell (due to his mysteriously disappearance).

"He's dead," they said.

This came as no great surprise as John had built the Hubbell House in 1854, but this perhaps indicated that time was not a concept in the spirit world.

I asked if he had died of natural causes (to try and eliminate the rumor of foul play).

"Yes," they replied.

"Is John here?" I continued.

"Yes," they said once more.

During this interaction I noticed a series of light anomalies moving around the theater seating. Heather proceeded to try and take photographs of the occurrence, but her camera refused to work. When she pressed the button, nothing happened and everything froze. I suggested that we ask for permission before taking a photograph; upon asking, the camera became operational again and the picture was taken. I also experienced a number of drains on my power packs and batteries during the vigil, affecting my camera, flashlight, thermometer, and ghost box (I have previously brought large car batteries to vigils to try and provide bigger sources of energy for entities).

A well-organized paranormal investigator is laden down with spare batteries of every size and shape, and is ready to use replacements at a moment's notice. It is worth mentioning that most investigations take place in cold, damp environments—atmospheres that would naturally cause batteries to fail or operate at a reduced rate—but the stage was not one of those environments.

I take photographs of the sites we investigate during the baseline tests and at the beginning of the vigils, to record where everything is positioned in the room; if during the course of the vigil objects move or appear, I have a visual record to refer to. Digital photographs allow me to document every aspect of the room and can be deleted if necessary after the evidence review. It has often proved advantageous to explain to the spirits that I am going to be taking a photograph and what that entails; I can then invite them to appear for me in a specific place before taking the picture—in the hope of getting them to pose. Disappointingly, no further contact could be made with Frank, Peter, or John.

Haunting in the Dressing Rooms

The dressing rooms are now located in three rooms on the second floor. They are strewn with the accoutrements of theater productions: rails of period costumes and hats fill the area; furniture is stacked to the ceiling; and the corridors are made narrow by the paintings that are stored on the floor. A macabre, deteriorating deer's head adorns a wall next to a stuffed fish—which appears to have been caught during the Paleozoic period. It looked like the union of a poorly maintained antiques shop, a costume emporium, and an underfunded natural history museum.

During the first vigil, in the basement, I became aware of the name *Cathy* being said inside my head over and over again; the name then evolved into *Catherine*. I dismissed this implanted psychic information at the time due to the success we were having with our equipment at that moment—but I decided to revisit this thought as I prepared for the third vigil. I saw in my mind a lady on her own, wearing a period dress of the early twentieth century, painting in detail the walls of the theater—I saw her painting landscapes and trees. I turned on the ghost box to see if this would be the catalyst for a dialogue with Catherine; the equipment started first by saying, "Hello."

"Hello," I said. "Is Cathy there?"

"Yes," she replied.

"Did you used to paint?"

"Paint," she repeated.

"Did you paint these walls or the set?" I inquired.

"Yes," she responded. "Yes, thank you."

"How old are you, Cathy?"

A response was made but was unintelligible (even on my recording equipment upon review).

"Robert," then came through in a man's voice.

It is common for multiple conversations to take place at once, as every entity present wants to communicate; spirits may have been residing for centuries in the hope of conveying a message—so one can understand their enthusiasm. Rightly or wrongly, it tends to be the spirit with the loudest voice that is heard. I try and avoid this scenario by asking them to appoint a spokesperson to talk on behalf of the group, so that some clarity might be brought to the information I am receiving. I also try to promote the idea of patiently waiting in line—this is my British nature coming through.

"How many of you are watching, Cathy?"

"Seven," she said, and then repeated, "Seven" again. (It appeared that one had left the location since Steve's vigil had taken place here.)

"How many are female?"

"Two," she responded—and repeated her answer another two times.

"Are you happy with me being here?"

"Yes," she said.

The name "Sorenson" was then heard twice in quick succession over the top of the dialogue; I asked if that was Robert again, but got no reply. I tried to encourage more dialogue by stressing that I would be leaving soon, and that this would be the last opportunity to make contact; I asked if there was something they would like to say.

"Yes," the ghost box said, followed by the word "Friends" a further two times.

"That is very kind of you," I responded. "I would love to be friends."

The ghost box then said, "Ghost."

"Are you a ghost?" I replied.

"Ghost—friend," it said back.

"Are you a friendly ghost?" I asked.

"Yes."

I don't normally use the term *ghost* when talking to an entity, because there is a possibility they may not know they are dead. I would never ask when or how they died for the same reason. On this occasion, however, the spirit led the conversation and gave me the word to use. I then said, "We really need to go."

It responded by saying, "Don't say that."

I asked if they were lonely and suggested there may be other places they could go.

"I'll wait for you," it said. This response was as loud and as clear as anything we had heard during our entire investigation. (I hoped that this was in reference to our next trip back to the Opera House—rather than after my demise.)

"We only have a few seconds left; what would you like to say?" I asked.

"Thank you," was the response, and with that I turned off the ghost box to end the investigation.

At the end of the night I asked Jane and Melisa if they knew a Catherine or a Robert Sorenson. They told me that Bob Sorenson was the original pianist for the Mantorville Theatre Company back in the 1970s—he had been dead for some considerable time. He was quite a character, and his piano playing was of the highest level; he once made a living from playing on transatlantic cruise ships.

Possessed Piano

The piano stands next to the steps that lead to the stage, ready and poised to be played at any moment as an accompaniment to a production. I left a DVR running on top of the piano throughout the entire course of the investigation. As I played the audio recording back (during the evidence review), I heard the piano being briefly played. My analytical and skeptical side wanted to believe that the lure of an open piano, with its sparkling-white ivory keys, was a temptation too great for any individual making their way through the auditorium onto the stage. It could also have been legitimately played by an investigator as a way of trying to promote contact with a spirit. Future investigations at the Opera House will involve placing the piano in a controlled area with motion sensors and trigger objects, to see if this phenomenon could be repeated.

CONCLUSION

The ghost-box evidence was certainly impressive, with the names of individuals coming through of which we had no prior knowledge. We did not access the ghostly actress, but it appears we may have made contact with two of the town's founders and touched upon the disappearance of John Hubbell—further investigations of the property would allow me to explore this in more detail and to tease out more information. I was also happy with my own contribution during the third vigil when I engaged with Catherine, initially through my clairvoyance and then via the ghost box.

The entire downtown area of Mantorville was added to the National Register of Historic Places in 1975, and the Opera House was deeded to the Mantorville Restoration Association at the beginning of the twenty-first century. The citizens of Mantorville are proud of their history and could not be more accommodating; they talk enthusiastically about their rich heritage, and many of the families can be traced back to the town's beginnings. It is a refreshing attitude towards my work and what I hope to achieve—not everyone is so open-minded in embracing me and my collection of odd equipment and strange nocturnal habits. It is only through prolonged visits and endless hours of investigation that all the details and evidence can be uncovered. I am confident with the support of the Opera House and the town I can start to fully understand the stories of Ellen, Catherine, and Bob, and perhaps provide the good people of Mantorville with more history to be proud of.

POSTSCRIPT

I had the privilege and opportunity recently to undertake a follow-up investigation at the theater. What I found to be impressive was the evidence I retrieved during the first vigil in the dressing room and storage area on the top floor. As soon as I had turned on the ghost box, a voice came through and said, "Is Adrian there?"

I replied, "Yes."

I inquired as to who was asking after me, and the spirit responded, "Bob."

I greeted Bob, and we proceeded to indulge in a conversation about what I had been doing since the last time we had met and how it was great to be talking with him again. It is an interesting concept to think that he remembered our previous conversation and came through to talk to me again at the first given opportunity—almost a year after our first meeting.

CHAPTER 9

LeDuc Historic Estate

HASTINGS

Séances, supernatural howling, and the ghost of a previous owner all suggest that the LeDuc Historic Estate does not just look haunted. It is haunted.

I have visited the LeDuc Historic Estate in Hastings, Dakota County, on two separate occasions, and the evidence that follows is a combination of those two investigations. I asked the manager of the estate if we could investigate in the building due to the tales I had heard about the ghostly activity there— the property is owned by the city of Hastings and is operated on their behalf by the Dakota County Historical Society; I also wanted to see inside the impressive façade that represents all the semiotics of an archetypal haunted house. Much of the source material for the research on the house came from online resources and was supplemented with information retrieved from period newspaper articles.

HISTORY

Set into a landscaped four-acre site, the LeDuc Estate provides an eye-catching mystique for all those traversing the Great River Road Scenic Byway; its resplendent, haunting silhouette has witnessed over a century of scared children running past the property on their way to school. This unique and nationally important Gothic Revival building is located on Vermillion Street (U.S. Highway 61), overlooking Hastings; it was the residence of William Gates LeDuc (1823–1917), a well-respected attorney, businessman, Civil War officer, and the Commissioner of Agriculture during the presidency of Rutherford B. Hayes (1877–81).

William's wife, Mary Elizabeth (1829–1904), chose the plans for the house from the seminal book *Cottage Residences*—written and published in 1842 by the renowned architect Andrew Jackson Downing. The style she picked was commonly known as Carpenter Gothic and represented a North American visual language of picturesque decorations applied to wooden buildings. The Gothic revival was implemented by Minnesota's carpenters, who facilitated the concept of the original intense and darker stone-built Gothic designs into the building process through the light-framed constructions of small domestic buildings and churches. The charm and quaintness of this style was emphasized by elaborate jig-sawn details—which were achieved through the invention of the steam-powered scroll saw and mass-produced wood moldings; this is observed through the pointed-arch windows, board-and-batten siding, and the towers, turrets, and steep gables. One of the most visible contributions of Downing's new inspired process was the front porch. Downing saw the porch as a gateway from the house into nature—and the new technological advances allowed the construction of porches onto new and existing buildings.

The LeDuc family moved into their newly built home in 1865, with their children Willie, Minnie, Florence, and later Alice; Mary LeDuc and her daughters soon became very active in the community and showed an interest in many topics, including Native American history and economics. Mary was never fully happy, however, and she documents in her journals a dislike of Hastings and the house—stating she was always unhappy about staying (it would be reasonable to believe that Mary would not be frequenting the house after her passing); she also wrote that she found Minnesota to be "cold and always blue."

ANDREW JACKSON DOWNING

Andrew Jackson Downing was born on October 31, 1815, and was one of the earliest and most influential landscape designers and horticulturists. Downing's vision was to see every American in possession of a good home, regardless of their income or social status. He thought that the moral education and philosophical outlook of America could be bettered and influenced by the interior designs and external appearance of the family home; he believed that people's pride in their country was connected to pride in their home. If they could decorate and build their homes to symbolize the values they hoped to embody—such as prosperity, education, and patriotism—

they would be happier and better citizens. Downing also believed that interacting with nature had a healing effect on the soul, and he designed his grounds accordingly; he did this by combining romanticist landscape features with the splendor of the English countryside.

Many Minnesotans were moving from the cities into the surrounding prairies in response to the introduction of the railroad. Many looked towards Downing's publications as a blueprint for their houses, from small, inexpensive detached wooden houses to the grander Gothic Revival mansions. His first book was called A *Treatise on the Theory and Practice of Landscape Gardening, Adapted to North America*, and was published in 1841. This was the first book of its genre published in the United States and became a great success. Downing next collaborated with Alexander Jackson Davis on the 1842 book *Cottage Residences*; this was an influential pattern book of twenty-eight affordable and simplistic house designs, complete with garden layouts and a plant guide. The book was widely consulted by Victorian builders, both commercial and private, and became instrumental in defining a stylistic vernacular that was embraced by all classes of society.

Downing's reputation grew throughout the 1840s as his designs dominated New York's Hudson River Valley. His new celebrity status and influence allowed him to campaign for a park to be constructed in New York City, which eventually led to the successful development of Central Park. Downing was approached to redesign and landscape the National Mall in Washington, D.C. His plan was for a classic geometrical design with curving walkways linking four separate park areas—replacing the traditional, central straight avenue—

and his ideas on structural planting provided a public, living gallery of plants, trees, and shrubs.

Downing was commissioned in 1851 to redesign the grounds for the White House, but unfortunately President Millard Fillmore and Congress saw Downing's designs as too expensive and withdrew his funding; Downing's plans were never brought to fruition at the White House and were only partially incorporated on the National Mall. Downing died on July 28, 1852, at the age of only thirty-six; he was killed with his wife and extended family while traveling on the steamship *Henry Clay* on the Hudson River. A boiler explosion onboard led to a fire that quickly enveloped the wooden vessel, resulting in the loss of eighty lives.

SPIRITUALISM AND SÉANCES

William LeDuc was intrigued by Spiritualism and held regular séances in the parlor and dining room of his home. Spiritualism developed throughout the latter half of the nineteenth century and reached its peak by the early twentieth century. It was said to have over eight million participants throughout the United States and Europe; many followers, like William, were drawn from the middle and upper classes. The rapping sounds, the playing of musical instruments, automatic writing, and divination appeared to present tangible evidence that practical-minded Americans found difficult to ignore.

The Ouija board as we know it, with its distinctive alphabet design and separate planchette, was not patented until 1890—but letters drawn on a table or a plate were used with a pendulum before this. It is believed William LeDuc used such a talking board during his séance sessions; it is possible that he opened up a window or a portal during his séances through which any number of spirits could have traveled without discrimination. It is therefore possible that the reported hauntings of the LeDuc house have no relation to the family or have no connection with the area or the house.

INVESTIGATION

I started the vigil in the parlor and called out into the cold, inky darkness that wrapped itself around us in an uncomfortable swirl; I asked if we were being observed and if the spirits could make themselves known to us. The rapping sounds that frequented the Victorian séances all those years ago rang out again for the first time since—in direct response. I asked for a second noise so I could try and discount a coincidental random noise; the same loud thump was heard again—someone or something wanted me to know they were there. I introduced technology to the vigil so I could have a more meaningful interaction with the entity; I asked the spirit via the ghost box how many spirits were in the room with us—and the answer came back instantaneously: "Eight."

To try and verify the response, I asked if they had said, "Eight." A young girl's voice once again said, "Eight."

It appeared that many spirits were residing in this building.

I then took the team into the dining room with a DVR and K2 EMF meter; the meter sat on the floor emitting a constant, small green light, providing the sole focus for my eyes in the void of blackness. I asked if the same person who had made the noise in the parlor would kindly move towards the green light, as a way of engaging with us further. In direct response to my question the meter ran across its range of readings from below 1.5 milligauss (through its illuminated diodes of green, yellow, and orange) before resting in the red of the highest reading, of over 20 milligauss. No further progress was made in this location, so we ventured upstairs.

The Spirit of William LeDuc

I set up our next vigil on the second floor—where the spirits appeared to be in a talkative mood; a nonstop stream of words spouted from the Ovilus at such a rate of speed that it was difficult to write them all down—I was grateful the session was being recorded. The word "Country" was said, and I asked if they remembered the country being at war during the Civil War. It replied by saying, "Epaulet."

An epaulet is an ornamental shoulder decoration used as insignia or rank by military forces. (This was a very strange word to come through, but we played the recording of the dialogue back on many occasions, and the whole team agreed that it clearly said, "Epaulet.") I was aware that William LeDuc was a brevet brigadier general, so I asked if I was speaking to William. The Ovilus then replied, "General."

I hoped that I had made contact with William LeDuc and asked for a clear response to my questions—was this William?

William Gates LeDuc came to Minnesota from Wilkesville, Ohio; he graduated from Kenyon College in 1848 and was admitted to the bar in 1849—he then came to settle in St. Paul. William soon found success in helping the Wabasha Bridge Company to facilitate the construction of the first bridge to span the Mississippi River, in 1853; he was also instrumental in organizing the first charter for a railroad through the territory. William joined the 11th Minnesota Infantry at Fort Snelling as a captain at the beginning of the Civil War in 1861; he quickly rose to the position of lieutenant colonel and chief quartermaster and developed a close association with the legendary generals W. T. Sherman, G. G. Meade, J. Hooker, and G. B. McClellan.

The quartermaster had the responsibility of supplying food, water, clothing, and transportation. William had to overcome the bureaucracy, the incompetence of fellow officers, and the logistical difficulties of supplying a Union Army on the move. During his command he became responsible for supplying the Army of the Potomac during the Peninsula Campaign and in providing food to stranded soldiers during the siege of Chattanooga; this he did by inspirationally commandeering a steamship. His exploits and memoirs are documented in the book *This Business of War: Recollections of a Civil War Quartermaster*. By 1865 William had risen to the position of brevet brigadier general of volunteers.

William's wheeling-and-dealing spirit, fine-tuned during the Civil War, was applied to his business ventures upon leaving the army; subsequently, in 1877, he was appointed as the U.S. Commissioner of Agriculture by President Rutherford B. Hayes—who recognized LeDuc's entrepreneurial nature. This position enabled William to promote homegrown teas and allowed him to become instrumental in providing plants and seeds to plantations in South Carolina and Georgia. He also oversaw the distribution process, making sure that the final product was sent to the most prominent and influential taste-testers. In 1880 Oliver Wendell Holmes, a personal family friend, and later a respected U.S. Supreme Court justice, described William as being one of biggest contributors in introducing tea culture to the New World. William LeDuc took his position seriously and promoted Minnesota at every given opportunity—including in what must have been one of the first public relations the state received:

> One of the first official attempts to advertise Minnesota was the Minnesota exhibit at a world's fair held in New York in 1853. The territorial legislature appointed William G. LeDuc to arrange for this exhibit and voted him three hundred dollars for expenses. It is interesting to know what LeDuc took with him to New York to give easterners an idea of Minnesota. He took an Indian canoe, some wild rice, some furs, grains raised on farms in southern Minnesota, a number of pictures, and—a live buffalo![32]

In 1878 William was indirectly brought to the attention of the press, when he found himself in the company of a less scrupulous businessman:

> Strange Doings—Some interesting developments relative to Rogers and LeDuc—How our Paternal President takes Care of his Friends. There have been for several weeks vague stories circulating about Private Secretary Rogers' business transactions in the northwest. First it has been stated that he was an old business associate of LeDuc, present Commissioner of Agriculture, and that they had taken advantage of certain of their creditors. This matter has culminated in a statement made to the President direct by Congressmen Lynde, of Wisconsin, in the shape of a claim preferred by Chandler & Brown,

commission merchants, of Milwaukee, for $1,750, a judgment having been procured for that amount. It has been stated that this debt was incurred by Rogers when in partnership with LeDuc.[33]

Unfortunately, William was mostly down on his luck when chasing his next dream, and the majority of his business dealings fell short of expectations; although when he was in his nineties (one year before he died), he finally gained the fortune he coveted when he received the sum of $100,000 from the spouse of an ex-business partner who had swindled him.

I asked additional questions with the Ovilus in the hope of engaging more with the entity; I tried desperately to get confirmation that we had made contact with William LeDuc, but this never came. What I did record though was one of the creepiest pieces of evidence I have ever obtained.

The Haunting Howl

It was during this possible interaction with William that the intensity of the moment was broken by what can only be described as a long, single-note wail of despair—a macabre howling that split the room in a two-second burst. It was the kind of noise that leaves the hairs on the back of your neck standing up; the team instantly agreed that the noise had come from the building rather than from an animal outside. I captured this desperate-sounding noise on my recording equipment, and it did not sound any less distressful on the second or third hearing; someone, somewhere was expressing their depression and unhappiness. It sounded exactly how you would expect a stereotypical ghost to sound (all that was missing was the sound of a rattling chain). Then the Ovilus said one final word:

"LeDue."

I thought it might be trying to say "LeDuc" and that I had misheard, but upon listening to the audio recording it definitely said "LeDue." I wondered if the entity was trying to say LeDuc, but it became distorted by the equipment in some way—like a misheard word on a long-distance phone call. No further contact was made in this location.

A Poltergeist in the Attic

I closed all the doors in the attic so that no light would bleed into the vigil area. Next, I conducted an EVP sweep and asked for a sign to see if any spirits were present. I became transfixed on the door to the hallway, hoping that an entity would stick to the laws of physics and use the door, rather than going through the wall, to engage with me. I was then startled by the sudden action of a light coming on behind me, fully illuminating the room—one of the table lamps placed on a bookshelf had inexplicably come on by itself.

At the end of the investigation I went back to the attic to retrieve my equipment; upon returning I noticed that one of the attic doors was now open—allowing a large amount of light to enter the room from the illuminated controls of the air conditioning unit that lay beyond it. This incident was significant because the room was in complete darkness until the lamp had come on; this meant that in the period between finishing the attic vigil and returning, the door had been opened. No members of the team had opened the door, and no one else was present in the building.

A Murder Mystery

It has become a familiar pattern that entities from previous investigations now engage with me on vigils in other buildings and in other parts of the state (physical distances do not apply to the spirit world); many of the details and conversations we have documented have started to bleed into one another—and the LeDuc Estate would prove to be an example of this.

A week before I investigated the LeDuc Estate we had the privilege of exploring the house of author Annie Wilder. Annie lives nearby and has written a book, *House of Spirits and Whispers*, about her experiences of living in a haunted house. During that investigation the spirit of a young girl named Emma made her presence known to us; she was very lucid via the ghost box. Emma claimed she was killed and buried face-down in the orchard of the LeDuc Estate—her comments were noted, and we hoped to explore them further during the LeDuc investigation.

The activity in the house appeared forthcoming and generally responded to most of our questions and requests; towards the end of the investigation I ventured to ask what the spirits knew of Emma—whom I believed to be interred within the grounds. The comment had the effect of pulling the plug on the rest of the investigation—everything appeared to leave me; not a single piece of evidence was received after this point. It would be easy to assume that this could be regarded as a "dirty secret" that no one wanted to talk about, even in the afterlife—or was this just purely coincidental?

Statistically, the majority of murders take place within the family, with the victim often related to the murderer. If Emma was buried within the grounds of the estate, it was possible that she was related to the LeDuc family. I decided to see if an Emma LeDuc was documented in any of the local period newspapers—I was hoping to find a story relating to her disappearance or murder. I found a single article for an Emma LeDuc who was a young student at Seward School; she had submitted a story to be published in the *Journal Junior* on June 14, 1902. I then decided to try and trace her on the 1900 Census, and I found that she had lived in Hennepin County in that year—having been born in August 1887.

At this point a very strange coincidence took place: on the census her name had been listed in two different ways; this is a common situation where the spelling of a name is hard to make out due to the scripted nature of the text on the original document, or because the scribe lacked writing skills. The other name she was listed under was "LeDue," the very name that had been said during the second-floor vigil.

Knowing that Emma's spirit had spoken of dying at a young age, I hoped to find her death certificate. I searched extensively, but I could not find any record of her death— perhaps suggesting that she disappeared, or never had her death officially documented (it is also possible that she was registered under a married name in later life). I then looked at the census details for 1910, because if she appeared on those I would know it was not the Emma I was looking for— but I found no record of her in the later census.

What I had discovered was a young girl with the name of Emma LeDuc/LeDue living relatively locally, who appears

to have disappeared sometime after 1902. She was last registered in ward twelve of Minneapolis. It is also worth noting that an orchard was part of the original footprint of the
LeDuc house. Much of the grounds were sold off over the
years, and other, more contemporary buildings now occupy
the land, covering over any possible grave. I recalled the
hauntingly depressing wail of a young girl that was heard
throughout the house.

All of these facts don't lead me any further along the path
of providing historical facts or proof of an afterlife, but investigating the paranormal will always offer more questions
than answers—and the whole scenario with Emma was very
intriguing.

I subsequently discovered another twist in the Emma
mystery—that William LeDuc's brother Charles had married an Emma Rachel Butler (this Emma was born in New
York on September 12, 1824). She married Charles in May
of 1855 and came to live in Hastings; Charles died in 1868,
and Emma remarried in 1873 to H. B. Claflin. This particular
Emma died at the age of eighty-eight in Covina, California,
on August 1, 1913.

Our ghost-box conversation evidence with Emma suggested that she was a child and died early under mysterious
circumstances, but it should be considered that Emma may
have had a daughter who was also named Emma, as it was
common practice during this period to name your eldest off-
spring after yourself.

What became more intriguing was the further discovery that Emma Butler's ashes were brought back to Hastings
from California, for burial at Lakeside Cemetery—but Lake-

side Cemetery has no record of her being interred there. Is it possible that her ashes were buried on the grounds of the LeDuc Estate, perhaps in the orchard? I wonder if that urn of ashes was accidently buried upside down.

CONCLUSION

The LeDuc family moved to a house in Minneapolis after William died in 1917, thirteen years after his wife, leaving the residence in Hastings solely as a summer house. By 1940 the LeDuc family sold the house to a close family friend, Carroll Simmons, who used the property as a base to run an antiques business. Simmons turned down a developer's $100,000 offer in 1957 to turn the home into a shopping center and instead donated the house to the Minnesota Historical Society the following year—in an agreement that allowed him to continue to live and operate his business there until he retired in 1986. The house then stood empty until 2002, when the Minnesota legislature released $1 million in bonding funds for the Historical Society to preserve the house, bringing it up to current building codes; further funds were raised in 2005 to restore the house and grounds to their former glory.

Our interaction with what I believe was William LeDuc was tantalizingly brief, and I would have wanted further evidence to confirm this fully. I believe that William's love of Spiritualism would mean that he would have tried his best to interact with us if he could—like he tried to contact spirits himself during the nineteenth century. The howl was one of the most bloodcurdling sounds I have ever heard and was very jolting at the time; the light coming on by itself in the attic would also suggest a strong paranormal presence in the property. It was disappointing to me that further conversations were not forthcoming from other members of the LeDuc household, but that may have been due to the knowledge I had brought with me of a possible family secret.

To help with their historical preservation, the National Register of Historic Places has listed many Carpenter Gothic buildings, but there are many more buildings that have not been recognized and are becoming increasingly endangered due to urban development. Many have also fallen into a state of disrepair and deterioration due to the nature of their wooden construction and Minnesota's harsh climate.

Other houses are literally picked up and relocated to new sites—which raises the question of whether a ghost would still frequent a house that has been moved from its previous location. Or do ghosts just roam in the space that the house vacated? The answer may depend on whether an entity is linked to the fiber of the building or the space. Perhaps a residual haunting would be more likely to be replayed in the area the incident took place, so would stay in that geographical location; but an intelligent haunting would, in a moment of sentience, realize the house was being moved—and hold on tight.

CHAPTER 10

The Wabasha Street Caves

St. Paul

The ghost of a murdered gangster and the spirit of a school-teacher are just a few of the numerous dead souls that regularly attend the events and celebrations at the caves—uninvited and normally unnoticed.

The Wabasha Street Caves have long been the subject of paranormal activity, and the owner, Donna Bremer, kindly agreed to give the team access to the location on several occasions. This property consists of seven caves and stands alone from the hundreds of unfinished and uninhabited caves along the river in St. Paul and Minneapolis—where teen deaths and cave-ins are sadly all too common. The majority of the historical information for the caves was uncovered from period newspapers at the Minnesota Historical Society in St. Paul; additional facts surrounding gangster involvement were accessed online and through the many publications that exist on their activities. Donna and the cave guides provided details that helped to focus my research further, including information on previous ghostly encounters and period photographs.

HISTORY

The seven caves on Wabasha Street South are located near the Mississippi River across from downtown St. Paul in what is referred to as the city's West Side. Although called caves, they are in fact mines that were first excavated out of the sandstone in the 1840s. Earlier settlers found that the soft sand gave way readily to the pick, and large underground caverns were soon created—the mined sandstone was used in the construction industry due to its strong resistance to weathering and its ability to be easily worked. The removed silica was also used in the production of windows, bottles, glasses, ceramic kitchenware, and later in the car-manufacturing industry.

Throughout their history the caves have been used for a number of different activities, ranging from the growing of mushrooms and the storage of food to the hosting of live music and dancing. The city authorities also tunneled farther into the rocks along the bluffs for drainage reasons; sandstone rock formations have unique properties that allow water percolation—subsequently, large quantities of water can be stored in the aquifers. As the *Saint Paul Daily Globe* put it in 1902:

> In every cave on the West side is to be found a well or cistern which never goes dry. Excavated a few feet in the rock, the constant seepage from the porous sandstone keeps a well constantly full.[34]

The Wabasha Street Caves, circa 1933

The majority of unoccupied and unfinished caves in St. Paul are located along Plato Boulevard and Water Street, and the public that passes the boarded-up entrances have little knowledge of their vast size. Some of the caverns and tunnels penetrate well under the plateau above and are divided into spacious rooms—although due to the threat of cave-ins, they are now partitioned into smaller areas than they were originally. Cave-ins are still frequent, but the caverns and tunnels are watched carefully, and any potential collapse is quickly detected and taken care of.

Many of the previous cave-ins have been documented: the Wabasha sewer collapsed in 1878 between Tenth Street and Exchange Street, and part of Wabasha Street caved in during 1886, when an infantry of Minnesota's K Company marched along it—with nine soldiers falling in. A further cave-in was reported in 1901, causing serious disruption along South Wabasha Street.

TRANSIENT SOULS

Until the late 1880s the caves along the Mississippi River bluffs of St. Paul lay idle and unused except for the bats and noisy nocturnal animals that resided there. Tumbledown houses then started to be built along the upper flats on the base of the great bluff, and some of their occupants used the caves to house their cattle and chickens. It then became a constant battle to keep this livestock away from the hungry stray dogs that took refuge there.

Occasionally, the homeless or transient population of St. Paul looked for shelter in these dark, wet dwellings. These unlucky souls added to the growing list of residual, paranormal negative energy of pain and anguish in this locality. Two articles from the *Saint Paul Daily Globe*, one from 1887 and the other from 1899, provide examples of this human desperation:

> The abodes of dogs and the shelter of tramps: Not far from under the Wabasha street bridge, a long, dark, unhealthy-looking hole in the ground, where rubbish has accumulated and where dogs have left the bones they took there to gnaw. They say a man, whose home no-one knew, whose relatives and friends, if he ever had any, had long since deserted him, lived seven days in that dark hole, with neither food nor drink. He had committed some crime and took this place of concealment. Remorse and fear so overcame him that he did not once venture towards the mouth of the little cav-

ern, but lay on the sand within, wasting away within fifty feet of where hundreds of people passed daily on the trains. He finally crawled out with his senses gone and climbed the bluff before throwing himself to his death, where he was found by a trackman who saw his emaciated body and assumed that he had been dead for sometime before being found.[35]

Carey Has A Chance For Life—Richard Carey, the aged man who took sulfuric acid in a cave under Wabasha street on Monday night, still survives at the city hospital, where it is said he will likely recover. Carey has given no other explanation for attempting to end his life further than that he was friendless and weary of living.[36]

The value of having large underground caverns in the West Side bluffs was first recognized and exploited by several small breweries. The Yoerg Brewery also utilized the local terrain on the southeast side of the river at the corner of Plato and Ohio—the caves provided an ideal location for the storage of beer during the fermentation process. Gradually, the number of rooms on the West Side increased until the caves finally encompassed the entire production of each brewery; the benefit of storing beer in this location came from the coldness it provided during the summer months. However, the extreme difference in temperature throughout the winter months was detrimental to the product. For this reason the breweries (including the Hamm brewery) constructed better regulated artificial cold-storage facilities elsewhere—as soon as the technology became available.

William Hamm saw the potential of using the vacated caves as the ideal environment for growing mushrooms; he was joined in this venture by a family of French immigrants who utilized an additional seven of the caves—and St. Paul soon became the mushroom capital of the Midwest, as it transported thousands of pounds of mushrooms all over the country.

CRUSHED TO DEATH

The threat of cave-ins continued into the twentieth century and became more prevalent as men started to work deeper inside the labyrinth of caverns and passages, toiling in poorly lit and confined areas while laying conduit for the Northwestern Telephone Company; incidents of near-misses and deaths were regularly documented in the local press:

> A St. Paul Avalanche—A stone wall at the Wabasha street embankment, West Side, caved in yesterday. One man was seriously injured; the other three had a narrow escape from instant death. Fifty tons of stone fell, and the workmen, stonemasons, who had been engaged repairing the wall, had to run for their lives. A heavy rock caught Anton Wietl, and his left arm and leg were injured.[37]

> Edward Mason killed by a caving while working on a steam shovel and instantly killed.[38]

A STORM OF PARANORMAL ACTIVITY

The Wabasha Street Caves were used at various times as a storage facility for the debris that had accumulated after a series of floods and storms. One infamous storm in 1904 caused many fatalities, adding to the long list of possible explanations for the paranormal activity associated with the Wabasha Street area. On August 20, a severe thunderstorm and tornado ripped through the city, destroying hundreds of buildings—resulting in $1,780,000 worth of damage (a considerable sum of money at the turn of the twentieth century). In downtown St. Paul a section of the High Bridge that spanned the Mississippi was blown down onto homes below—resulting in the loss of three lives and over fifty injuries. During this storm the U.S. Weather Bureau anemometer (which was positioned on the top of the *Pioneer Press* building) recorded a constant, sustained, one-minute wind speed of 110 miles per hour with a gust speed of 180 miles per hour—these readings still hold the record for the highest-ever documented wind speed in Minnesota. It is possible that higher measurements could have been recorded during this storm, but the equipment was then torn from the roof and never seen again.

Flooding was cyclical in St. Paul, and rarely would a five-year gap pass without the Mississippi breaking its banks—sweeping everything away in its path. Two of the caves were utilized to store the rubbish from the aftermath of the destruction. They have never been emptied, and you can still witness the detritus of rusting bed frames, wardrobes, street furniture, doors, and twisted construction materials. I suspect that some of those items have negative energies attached to them—from the poor souls who once owned them.

Much of the debris deposited in the caves came from the great flood of April 1952, when unseasonably wet weather created one of the worst floods ever seen in Minnesota. Hundreds of acres of upriver farmland were already underwater when the Mississippi finally burst its banks in downtown St. Paul on the 9th—with water rising at a rate of over an inch every hour. The Red Cross stepped in to lead the relief effort as large portions of the lower West Side had to be evacuated, leaving approximately 2,641 families temporarily homeless. On the 13th, flood levels were recorded at 20.4 feet; this broke the previous record of 19.7 feet set in 1881. By the 15th, every lowland dwelling from Fort Snelling to Inver Grove was underwater.

PROHIBITION

In the 1920s an area of the caves was developed as an amateur nightclub and restaurant; this became known as the Wabasha Street speakeasy (with its own whiskey still). This underground venue became a haven for the middle classes of St. Paul, who mingled shoulder to shoulder with the local gangsters and criminals; it would be easy to believe that these gangsters would bring negativity with them in the same way outlaws had in the previous century. As historian Theodore Blegen writes in his book *Building Minnesota*:

> The 1920s were a period of national prohibition. The state in 1921 passed strict laws to enforce the national prohibition amendment. There were many federal enforcement officers in the state, including Andrew Volstead, for whom the prohibition law had been named the Volstead Act. A border patrol tried to prevent people from smuggling liquor into the state. In

Minnesota, as in the nation at large, it was hard to enforce the prohibition law. Federal agents in Minnesota in 1929 seized more than 235,000 gallons of liquor and 271 stills. Underworld rings fought to control the illegal trade. So the attempt to prohibit drinking ran its course.[39]

By the late 1920s local authorities had started to turn a blind eye to the sale and production of alcohol. Prohibition was beginning to look like a failed policy, and those policing it were reluctant to enforce it. With the ratification of the Twenty-first Amendment, Prohibition came to an end in 1933. William and Josie Lehmann decided to make the speakeasy a more professional legal establishment (Josie was the daughter of the French family that had originally started mushroom farming in the caves); in late 1933 the Castle Royal was opened for business.

This new establishment was a high-end nightclub that boasted a bar, card-playing area, kitchen, liquor storage facilities, and a reception room, dance floor, and stage. An elegant dining room allowed patrons to enjoy a delicious meal (one dollar was charged for dinner) before dancing to the sounds of the touring big bands that filled the stage with a cacophony of gleaming brass instruments, penetrating the smoky atmosphere with music of the swing jazz era. The musicians played long into the morning above a thronging sea of dancers, all making use of the 1,600 square feet of dance floor. Cards could also be played next to an open fire (this area could also act as the warm accompaniment to shady business transactions).

INVESTIGATION

A Gangster Ghost

The small card room leads from the main cave area and was once the location for the darker side of the criminal underworld. Four gangsters were playing cards next to the fire, enjoying the libations and live music, exchanging money on the turn of a card. A large-framed man carrying a case then came into the Castle Royal and accosted the bandleader, suggesting to him (rather menacingly) that the band quit for the night, due to unfinished business he had to take care of; under the circumstances the bandleader took the man's advice and played one last song before packing up.

Shortly afterwards the patrons drifted out—leaving just the four card players, the large man carrying the case, and an impatient waitress waiting to lock up. The waitress retired back into the kitchens and proceeded to hear the recognizable sound of a Tommy gun—short bursts of loud, repetitive popping; it was said that the Tommy gun was the sound that had made the Twenties roar, and that night such a gun was roaring very loudly indeed.

After a period of silence the waitress crept nervously back into the card room, where she was greeted by the scene of three dead, distorted, and broken card players—a seeping puddle of the darkest red blood was also inching its way across the floor towards her shoes. The man with the case and the fourth card player (believed to be his accomplice) had both vanished. The waitress called the police, who arrived promptly. They asked her to step outside as they dealt with the crime scene.

After a considerable period of time the police returned to the waitress, and asked her why she had wasted their time with the false reporting of a murder. They asked her to retract her story under the threat of prosecution; the police were claiming that no sign of a crime had taken place. She insisted on going back inside the Castle Royal and refused to be intimidated; she took the police officers back inside, but to her surprise the bodies were gone—all signs of the crime had been removed. The waitress was adamant, however, and refused to accept the situation. She showed the police the bullet holes left in the soft sandstone walls—which graphically spelled out the night's events.

The intrigue of that night may never be fully known, but it is theorized that the large hit man and his accomplice may not have fled the scene; as the waitress tried to contact the police, they may have removed the bodies to the farthest disused parts of the cave to dispose of them. It is also possible that police undertook this task to brush the night's events under the carpet; gangsters killing gangsters meant fewer crimes and fewer criminals to investigate.

As the team came into this area, Steve R. proceeded to take a series of baseline photographs; orbs were present in most of the pictures—although these anomalies were nothing more than the water vapor in the damp cave air bouncing the flash back to the camera. As we investigated the room we ran multiple DVRs that provided us with some interesting evidence during the audio review; at the start of proceedings you can clearly hear Steve R., the team leader, ask, "Are you ready to start?"

To which a spirit responded, "Yeah, we are."

This response gave me the sense that the spirits were willing to respond (in a positive or negative way) and that there were multiple entities—due to the use of the word *we*. Just then Steve R. noticed what appeared to be a dark shadow of someone bending down; he saw the side view of a head and shoulders in a bent position—perhaps looking towards the floor or bent double in pain from a gunshot (the apparition disappeared as quickly as it arrived). It could be argued from a psychological viewpoint that Steve R. wanted to see the gangster appear so had become more open to the suggestion of shapes and shadows resembling this. The Ovilus repeated the same three words in quick succession, "Murder, dirt, dug," during this incident, adding more validity to the sighting; this is particularly intriguing when you consider that the three dead gangsters are believed to be buried at the back of the caves. Individual evidence of paranormal activity is always strengthened if presented with information from other sources and technology.

In the late 1930s the Castle Royal was closed, and a few years later the interior was again turned over to mushroom production in a bid to help the war effort. In the 1970s a new dance club and bar opened: the Castle Royal 2; this became the local center for a new dance craze called disco. This new enterprise did not stop the gangsters from frequenting their favorite haunt though. A young employee was closing up the venue after a night's entertainment, when he suddenly witnessed the figure of a man walking towards him wearing the apparel of a 1920s gangster—with a pin-striped suit and trilby hat; the employee never thought for one moment that it could possibly be a ghost, as the figure looked completely lifelike. He thought initially that a customer was wearing a theatrical costume, but the scary-looking character had cold eyes and a hostile demeanor. The ghost then walked straight past him and disappeared through the wall.

In the 1980s, after the demise of disco, the caves were renamed as the Library and became a teen nightclub—open every Thursday to Sunday night (it was called the Library so teenagers could inform their parents that they were going to the library). One of the investigation team, Erin, said she had worked there during this time and confirmed to me that she had seen the gangster apparition around the area of the fireplace; she also recalled hearing voices and seeing strange shadow figures at the back of the cave (just as Steve R. had done). She also experienced the frustration of objects going missing, only to find them again in weird places; it certainly adds more weight to the suggestion that the caves are a place of paranormal activity when a member of the investigation team can personally corroborate such activity.

The caves are now a venue that boasts a floor space of over 12,000 square feet; this includes a theatrical stage, a hardwood dance floor, a carpeted dining area, a cocktail room, and an expansive sixty-foot bar. The hallways emphasize the caves' gangster tradition by displaying framed photographs of 1930s criminality; these pictures have also been the target of paranormal activity and are often found hanging upside down.

John Dillinger

Some of the more notorious gangsters are said to have frequented the caves during its boom period; it is rumored that

John Dillinger (1903–34) danced the night away with various women at the nightclub. On one occasion he asked a young lady to dance. After they had finished, Dillinger left, and the lady was asked by the barman if she knew who the gentleman was. She was shocked to discover that she had danced with America's biggest public enemy.

Dillinger only spent a limited amount of time in the area though; he came to St. Paul with his girlfriend Evelyn "Billie" Frechette after robbing a bank in Mason City, Iowa, in 1934—once in St. Paul they teamed up with Lester "Baby Face" Nelson, Homer Van Meter, Eddie Green, and Tommy Carroll. Dillinger arranged accommodation at the Lincoln Court Apartments on Lexington Parkway South, under the pseudonym of Mr. and Mrs. Carl Hellman. The manager of the apartments soon became suspicious of the couple, however, due to their insistence on using the rear entrance and staying inside for the majority of their stay (they also refused to allow the apartment's caretaker into their room). The manager decided to report them to the authorities, and on March 30, 1934, the FBI began a surveillance operation.

The following morning two FBI agents (joined by Detective Henry Cummings of the St. Paul Police Department) knocked on their door; the reply came from Frechette—she kept them waiting behind the door by claiming she needed to get dressed. As the agents waited, Homer Van Meter appeared in the stairway on his way to the apartment; he was questioned briefly before he drew his gun—a firefight ensued in the hallway. Dillinger then spat sporadic machine-gun fire through the crack in the apartment door before breaking into the hallway under a hail of bullets—he raced down the back emergency stairwell and into his car. Van Meter also fled back down the stairs and forced a truck driver at gunpoint to drive to Green's apartment. The FBI called for backup but it was too late—they had already fled. Dillinger and Frechette also made their way to Green's apartment. Dillinger was given rudimentary treatment for a bullet wound he received to his leg during the escape—he had been shot by Cummings with a .38 Hand-Ejector 1905 Smith & Wesson revolver. (This weapon is now displayed by the Minnesota Historical Society.)

The FBI searched the smoking apartment as the smell of burnt gunpowder hung heavy in the air—they found a Thompson (Tommy) submachine gun with the stock removed, two automatic rifles, one .38 caliber Colt automatic with twenty-shot magazine clips, and two bulletproof vests. On April 3 the FBI tracked down Green's hideout; as they approached, Green drew his gun but was shot down before he could discharge his weapon—he died in a hospital eight days later. Dillinger and Frechette moved to another apartment in St. Paul, but on April 9 the authorities discovered the pair again; Dillinger had to look on from a block away as federal agents led Frechette away from their latest hideout. Dillinger was restrained by a companion, who convinced him that any attempt to retrieve her would result in his death.

Dillinger found himself racing back to St. Paul on April 22, in a 1930 Ford Model A, after engaging in a gunfight in a wood in Wisconsin (an agent and an innocent bystander were shot dead during this encounter). Dillinger was now accompanied by the gang members Van Meter and John "Red" Hamilton; they were coming back to Minnesota so

Dillinger could be closer to where the police were holding Frechette.

They got as far as Hastings when they became embroiled in a gun battle for the second time; Hamilton was shot in the back during this engagement, but they still managed to fashion an escape, and they retreated back to Chicago. Here they met up with members of the Barker-Karpis gang, in a bid to find medical treatment for Hamilton (who subsequently died from his wounds on April 27). Dillinger must have been impressed with his Ford Model A, because after his escape from Minnesota he sent a letter to Henry Ford—postmarked from Minneapolis on May 6, 1934 (suggesting that he came back again for a final time). In the letter Dillinger expressed his thanks to Ford for being able to outrun the police and FBI cars. Just a month later, however, Dillinger was shot dead by federal agents outside a theater in Chicago. Frechette served two years and one day under the federal harboring law at a federal corrections facility in Michigan.

There is no firm evidence (other than hearsay) to suggest that Dillinger actually frequented the caves. During his visit to St. Paul in March 1934 he was hiding from the authorities and keeping a low profile—his landlord, after all, became suspicious because he never left the apartment. Dillinger had a close relationship to Evelyn Frechette during this time—he actually swore to protect her if she promised she would never run out on him, so a solo nightclub visit involving dancing with other women appears unlikely. The next occasion he was near St. Paul was when he was fleeing from the failed arrest attempt in Wisconsin—which resulted in the two killings. At that time Dillinger was being chased by a posse of federal agents and was nursing a badly shot colleague—I suspect a nightclub visit would not have been high on his list of priorities then either.

If you wanted to embrace the romantic notion of Dillinger drinking and dancing the night away at the caves, you could point to the fact that the Lincoln Apartments were only eleven miles from the Castle Royal. Dillinger also had access to a car, and his swashbuckling nature would have perhaps enticed him into a risky public appearance. He was also present in Minneapolis at the beginning of May 1934, when he had time to compose and mail the letter to Henry Ford.

Frechette actually met Dillinger in a dance club, where he approached her and bought her a drink, so he was not opposed to approaching women in the manner the legend would have us believe. Of course gangsters do not want their whereabouts documented and try not to leave a trail for the authorities (or historians, for that matter) to follow; so the legend of Dillinger frequenting the caves can probably never be proved or disproved—unless, of course, he wanted to pay me a paranormal visit.

"Ma" Barker

Kate "Ma" Barker (1873–1935) was another high-profile recidivist that legend suggests graced the nightclub. Ma Barker left Missouri and traveled north to St. Paul on several occasions—the city had a lenient policy towards criminals hiding from the law. Her boys did not stay idle though, and on December 16, 1932 (along with associate Alvin Karpis) robbed the Northwestern National Bank—killing a policeman in the process. The following summer Ma Barker and the gang were back, but this time with grander schemes of kidnapping. On June 15, 1933, they undertook the kidnapping of William Hamm from outside of his brewery in the hope of securing a large ransom; there is every possibility that the Barker boys witnessed Hamm frequenting the area around the caves as part of his business ventures, and they may have even formulated their plans in the Wabasha Street Caves. Hamm was taken to Chicago, and a ransom was duly paid; this involved a package of cash being thrown from a moving car on a deserted road in St. Paul.

Feeling buoyed by the success of their kidnapping, the Barker-Karpis gang returned to St. Paul to follow their tried and tested policy of bank robbery. On August 10, 1933, they successfully stole the payroll at Stockyards National Bank of South St. Paul; a policeman lost his life during the heist and another was seriously injured. A second kidnapping was undertaken in St. Paul on January 17, 1934; this time they targeted Edward George Bremer, the son of the owner of another prosperous brewery, the Schmidt Brewing Company. This would prove to be the gang's undoing, and we shall learn of their misfortune during the Schmidt Brewery investigation in chapter 13.

Even less likely is the idea that Ma Barker found herself in the caves; a sixty-one-year-old farmer's wife from Missouri in an expensive avant-garde jazz swing bar seems unlikely. Her role within the gang was purely to look after the boys, and she was often sent to the movies when the gang went about its illegal activities. The gang never included her in their business plans and would make sure nothing was discussed around her; it is therefore more likely

The stage area in the Wabasha Street Caves

that Alvin Karpis and the Barker boys came to the Castle
Royal to discuss the kidnappings away from her and to while
away the periods of inactivity.

The Uninvited Wedding Guests

The caves are now used for wedding receptions and other
celebratory events, but the haunting continues despite the
change in décor. During one wedding reception, a small boy
in attendance was asked by his mother if he had enjoyed that
evening's events; the boy replied that he enjoyed playing
with the men at the table. His mother made the assumption
that the boy was referring to the employees who had dressed
for the event in the style of gangsters, but the boy insisted
they were not members of staff. When the bride and groom
developed their photographs, there appeared to be a heavy,
ghostly mist surrounding the boy; one image was particularly

intriguing as it showed the boy sat at a dining table playing, surrounded on both sides by foggy entities—it was assumed they were the men the boy was referring to.

In 1994 a child once again became witness to a ghostly experience. While the owners were in the process of cleaning the caves, their young son was occupying himself by bouncing a ball against a wall—and the ball happened to roll past an open door into the men's restroom. The boy chased after it and was startled to see a gangster looking in the mirror, adjusting his tie; the figure then turned and smiled at the boy before disappearing. The boy ran out in a fit of terror. This experience would suggest the haunting is intelligent, as the entity acknowledged the boy.

The Spirit of Harriet Bishop

During our walkthrough, the name "Harriet" was said by the Ovilus during a team discussion about nearby Harriet Island (it is a frequent phenomenon that spirits start to interact when a dialogue takes place between team members—many EVPs have been captured during downtime when investigators are talking about everyday topics). We noted that the catalyst for hearing the name was the mention of the island and continued to explore the caves. Then, throughout the course of the night, the name Harriet was mentioned separately on two additional occasions. Harriet could not be considered a common name, and due to the frequency of the times it was uttered I felt it was worthy of further investigation—I had never heard the Ovilus ever say this name before. The team never managed to engage with Harriet, but she was definitely informing us of her presence. I knew nothing about who or what Harriet could be, so I looked into the significance of Harriet Island—this proved to be a starting point in unraveling the mystery (it was an example of where the paranormal world starts to inform the direction of the historical research).

Harriet Island is a small landmass in the Mississippi across from downtown St. Paul, close to the caves. It was named after Harriet E. Bishop (1817–83). The pavilion on the island was originally called the Harriet Island Pavilion but was renamed the Clarence W. Wigington Pavilion after a restoration in 2000 (Wigington was the nation's first African American municipal architect). Harriet Bishop traveled from the East Coast to the embryonic town of St. Paul in 1847 after having taught school in New York State for several years. St. Paul at this time was just a frontier outpost with few redeeming features; the entry about Bishop in the book *Notable American Women 1607–1950* describes what the community was like when Bishop arrived:

> She arrived in mid-July in St. Paul, then a primitive trading post among the Sioux Indians consisting of a few log structures and containing at most twenty families, of which three were American.[40]

She was brought to Minnesota as part of a missionary education program led by educational reformer Catherine Beecher—this involved sending female teachers to frontier towns to "civilize" and educate their children. St. Paul was seen as a rough, recidivist town and was operating outside of the normal frameworks of society. Harriet described her difficult journey and her early thoughts about St. Paul in her journal:

This was the first I had heard of St. Paul, or even of Minnesota, and the impression was at once riveted on my mind that I must go; and when, after two weeks of prayerful deliberation, the question was asked, "Who will go to St. Paul?" I could cheerfully, though tremblingly, respond, "Here am I; send me." Every possible obstacle was presented; the difficulties of the almost unknown route; the condition of society; doubts as to a welcome by the people generally; the self-denials to be exercised; the privations to be endured—all of which were to me as so many incentives to persist in my decision. In short, I came because I was more needed here than at any other spot on earth, and because there was no other one of my class who felt it a duty to come.

My present residence is in the utmost verge of civilization in the northwestern part of the United States, within a few miles of the principal village of white men in the territory that we suppose will bear the name of Minnesota, which some would render, "clear water," though strictly, it signifies slightly turbid or whitish water.[41]

Her remit also included exerting her moral influence on the rough frontier town; Harriet did this by engaging in issues of temperance, educational reform, and women's suffrage. Harriet wrote extensively of her thoughts and experiences, and these notes were eventually published into a text called *Floral Home*. This book provides a unique insight into the lives of the earliest known white explorers and settlers to the region. Harriet also talks of her encounters with Native

Americans and the interaction that took place between them and the earliest pioneers arriving in Minnesota.

Harriet instigated the first-ever school in St. Paul, teaching children of every creed, race, and nationality; she also started the first Sunday school, which led to the building of the first Baptist church. You can see Harriet starting to form the ideas of developing a school in her journal comments; she has also started to observe the overabundance of, and reliance on, alcohol by the local population:

> The village referred to has grown up within a few years in a romantic situation on a high bluff of the Mississippi, and has been baptized by the Roman Catholics by the name of St. Paul. They have erected in it a small chapel, and constitute much the larger portion of the inhabitants. The Dakotas call it Im-mi-ja-ska (white rock), from the color of the sand-stone which forms the bluff on which the village stands. This village has five stores, as they call them, at all of which intoxicating drinks constitute a part, and I suppose the principal part, of what they sell. I should suppose the village contains a dozen or twenty families living near enough to send to school. Since I came to this neighborhood, I have had frequent occasion to visit the village, and have been grieved to see so many children growing up entirely ignorant of God, and unable to read his Word, with no one to teach them. Unless your Society can send them a teacher, there seems to be little prospect of them having one for several years. A few days since I went to the place for the purpose of making inquiries in reference to

the prospect of a school. I visited seven families, in which there were twenty-three children of proper age to attend school, and was told of five more, in which were thirteen more that it is supposed might attend, making thirty-six in twelve families. I suppose more than half of the parents of these children are unable to read themselves and care but little about having their children taught. Possibly the priest might deter some from attending, who might otherwise be able and willing.[42]

Harriet developed a strong involvement with the temperance movement; she believed in prohibition and urged for a reduction in alcohol sales and against excessive alcohol use. She campaigned tirelessly for complete abstinence and pressured the government to enact anti-alcohol legislation. Her domineering and forceful personality was applied to these ambitions, as is noted in the book *Notable American Women*:

Quick in speech and in resolute in action, she attacked issues on their merits alone, thereby frequently alienating the timid. She was particularly zealous in her struggle to advance the temperance movement.[43]

After uncovering Harriet Bishop's strong beliefs and moral crusading towards the selling and consumption of alcohol, and noting her assiduity towards the moral education of St. Paul, it would not be unreasonable to suggest that she now frequents the caves in spirit—especially as she lived, worked, and died so close to the location (she is buried in Oakland Cemetery in St. Paul). In her lifetime she would have seen the caves around St. Paul used as a storage facility for the brewing industry, and then in spirit for the flouting of prohibition laws married with gangster activities; this would certainly have brought a strong reaction from her. This may account for the phenomenon of objects going missing; perhaps it's a tactic she employs to hinder the smooth running of the caves.

CONCLUSION

Unfortunately, deaths are still prevalent in the caves that litter themselves along the Mississippi from St. Paul to Minneapolis; many teenagers continue to die from the result of carbon monoxide poisoning after making fires in the back of the caves. This happened in 1995, when two teenagers died after lighting a fire for heat and light; this unfortunate incident was then repeated on April 27, 2004, when three more teenagers died. The city of St. Paul has attempted to prevent cave intrusion by posting warning signs and obstructing entrances, but those with enough determination can still gain access. Once a fire is lit, the other sealed entrances actually exacerbate the situation by reducing the ventilation; the wood used to board up the entrance also gets burned as firewood. There have been so many violent deaths and related incidents throughout these caves that it would be reasonable to suggest that paranormal activity would be present in them and the surrounding area.

The only deaths believed to have taken place directly at the Wabasha Street Caves were those of the gangsters, but unfortunately no contact was made with them during our time there. However, a team member had seen one ghostly criminal gentleman previously—and I have no reason to disbelieve her.

The continual use of the word *Harriet* throughout my time at the caves was an interesting development, as its significance was not known to me at that moment and was only discovered through research after the event.

CHAPTER 11

The Old Jail and Saloon

TAYLORS FALLS

Strange smells, the spirit of a steamship captain, and the tragic death of a child are all imprinted into the cell walls of the Old Jail and Saloon.

I asked to investigate at the Old Jail and Saloon in Taylors Falls after reading about the hauntings that take place there. These buildings are now part of a B & B, and are an area rich with history and paranormal activity. We investigated during a single visit, and I organized teams to undertake vigils in different parts of the property at the same time.

Historical details about the area and the building were obtained through period newspaper articles archived by the Minnesota Historical Society. In 1981 the site became the Old Jail Bed & Breakfast (Minnesota's first licensed B & B), complete with a loft bedroom, wood-burning stove, and paranormal activity. Guests can now be awakened by strange supernatural white lights that illuminate the bedroom. The owner, Don Lawrence, and property manager, Kate Holland, also have extensive knowledge of the site and very kindly gave me historical photographs to use in my research. I also accessed many online resources and used the Old Jail website as a useful starting point.

HISTORY

Taylors Falls nestles on the banks of the St. Croix River on the eastern edge of the state, in Chisago County, and is one of the oldest towns in Minnesota; this location was first traversed and mapped in 1680 by the French soldier and explorer Daniel Greysolon (1639–1710). Three years later, Father Louis Hennepin documented that Greysolon had witnessed, on the banks of this site, the burial of an American Indian who had died of a rattlesnake bite. Hennepin then named what is now the St. Croix River the "River of the Tomb" (*Rivière Tombeaux*). Death was prevalent during this period, and place names were often based on events that had occurred at a particular site.

In September 1838 the Ojibwe Indians signed a paper, the *Dodge Treaty*, which was ratified by the United States Congress—this event allowed white settlers to legally access the St. Croix River Valley for the first time. That year Jesse Taylor (a Kentucky-born pioneer working as a stonemason at Fort Snelling) traveled up the St. Croix at the head of a steamship navigation with Benjamin Baker—access was only possible from the St. Croix River by steamship, birch-bark canoe, or barge. They staked a claim on the west bank of the river—

The Old Jail, Taylors Falls (Photo by Ron Jamiolkowski)

where a sole French fur trader named Robinet was living in a makeshift shanty. Baker and Taylor could envisage the huge commercial benefits the abundant spread of virgin white-pine forests could provide; they began the construction of a sawmill and called their encampment *Baker's Falls*.

In 1846 they sold their stake to Joshua Lovejoy Taylor (no relation) for $200. Joshua and his brother Nathan were lumber merchants from Sanbornton, New Hampshire, and they wanted to develop the fledgling town further. The brothers surveyed the area fully in 1851 and laid down the first plat, which they called *Taylor Place*. Nathan then established a post office in the same year. W. H. C. Folsom soon joined them and opened a general store (the rapids prohibited steamships from progressing farther up the river, thus supplying a ready-made clientele of loggers and crews requiring provisions before moving west). Folsom went on to become one of the most cel-ebrated citizens of Taylors Falls—as illustrated by his obituary from 1900:

> Dec 17—Hon. W. H. C. Folsom died Saturday night at
> 10 o'clock. Mr. Folsom sustained an attack of paralysis
> about a month ago, and his advanced years precluded
> recovery—interment will be at Taylor's Falls. Mr. Fol-
> som was the author of one of the most exact histories
> of the state, 'Fifty Years in the Northwest.' At one time
> he served as state senator, and also nearly approached
> the nomination for the governor in a Republican con-
> vention.[44]

THE GHOSTLY STEAMSHIP CAPTAIN

It is believed the spirit of a steamship captain still frequents the old saloon building—perhaps he is patiently enjoying a drink as Mr. Folsom assembles the supplies he needs. Sev-eral people have recently reported seeing and smelling cigar smoke, mixed with the recognizable aroma of sulfur matches; they believe he lights up in what is now the B & B office, before wandering through to the living room to smoke.

A bridge spanning the St. Croix River was completed in 1853; during its construction a crude government road was cut through to the town—connecting Taylors Falls with Still-water, Point Douglas (near Hastings), and Lake Superior. The surrounding forests were so impenetrably thick that settlers required an axe to make any kind of progress—they even had to leave markers so they could find their way out again. It was then possible to reach Taylors Falls by foot or on horseback, but the trail remained treacherous for unsuspecting travelers picking a path through the dense, dark forestation that enveloped the settlement. Whirlpools from glacial rivers flowed violently through this area during the Ice Age, leaving large holes drilled into the bedrock; this created the world's biggest glacial pothole at sixty feet deep—not a geographical feature you would want to stumble across in the dark. Access to Taylors Falls improved steadily throughout the latter part of the nineteenth century with investment obtained due to its economic growth:

> Commissioner Brown offered the following resolution: that $150 is appropriated for the Minneapolis & Taylors Falls road.[45]

The town quickly became populated with immigrants who decided to stay after traversing the river—the majority of whom were Swedish; this convention continued when the railroad replaced the steamship as the primary entry to the town:

> Taylors Falls Journal: Immigrants are passing by the train load, and a goodly number are dropping off in this region.[46]

Relatives of the author Vilhelm Moberg were among these early settlers in 1851; decades later, their stories gave Moberg, who was born in 1898, the inspiration to write and form the characters for his tetralogy, *The Emigrants*. Swedish immigrants had been arriving in America for many centuries—a colony was established as far back as 1638 by Queen Christina of Sweden; this was an official territory of the realm of Sweden in the Delaware Valley. Immigration from Sweden did not reach its peak until the 1890s, however, and in 1896 the Vasa Order of America, a Swedish fraternal organization, was established to help Swedes in America.

The majority of Swedes arrived at the harbors of New York City and Boston, and many then took the train on to St. Paul, at a time when the Great Northern Railway was eating its way through the vast expanse of prairie. Early immigrant pioneers arrived by stone-boat, sledge, and with ox teams—many of them took stock from St. Paul before pushing on to Taylors Falls.

THE GHOST OF ETTA

No town could profess to be habitable until a proper saloon was in place, and in 1851 Frank and Joseph Schottmuller (from Baden, Germany) took up the mantle in Taylors Falls. The financial rewards where obvious, as a supply of thirsty, trapped loggers waited eagerly to embrace their wares. They started building into the hillside between the St. Croix River and the Angel Hill area on Government Street. The construction was erected above a cave so the brothers could use the natural features of the land to keep their barrels cool and well stored—this became known as the Cave Saloon and was run by Peter Trump. The saloon was an immediate success. Times were harsh and relief was regularly sought at the end of a bottle, so the brothers expanded their operations further in 1862:

> The Schottmuller Brothers have their new brewery in operation. It is of gigantic proportions, is calculated for offensive operations upon all sides, and is said to be a dead shot to the "blues."[47]

The current owner, Don Lawrence, believes that a spirit named Etta resides in the saloon; he informed me of several ghostly encounters that have occurred around the process of housekeeping. Etta Hovey was married to Frank Schott-muller, and their wedding was documented in the *Minneapolis Journal*:

> Taylors Falls—Frank Schottmuller and Etta Hovey were married at the residence of the bride's parents yesterday afternoon. They were reared here and are popular. The wedding was attended by many friends and relatives from the state and Wisconsin.[48]

Etta's presence is often felt in the small bedroom and the blue room, where she slept; a staff member described to me the experiences she had encountered in these rooms.

One morning she had just finished making the bed in the smaller room, leaving the covers and pillows fluffed up; upon her return, less than an hour later, she discovered a person-shaped indentation on the bed—clearly showing where the arms, legs, and torso had rested (no guests were present at this time). This experience was repeated for a second time in the loft of the jailhouse, as the bed was being made when two large, palm-shaped indentations appeared on the covers—as though someone had leaned forward and rested with their arms; this all happened within the time it took her to turn and retrieve a comforter from the rail. Several staff members have also smelled the scent of strong perfume in the small sitting area called the "overlook"—and this has also been attributed to Etta.

THE SPIRIT OF FRANK

During my research on the Schottmuller family, I discovered that Frank and Etta had a total of four children. To my astonishment I found that their second son, Frank Everett (1908–10), died as a child from the effects of eating sulfur kitchen matches; this may account for the recognizable smell of sulfur that penetrates the air in the old saloon area (where they lived). This could then be combining with the smell of the cigar-smoking captain, leading people to believe that he lights up his cigar in one room and smokes it in another—when in fact they are two separate smells caused by two separate spirits. It is possible that Frank and the captain arrive together, though in different places, because the atmospheric conditions in the building are right for them to manifest at that time.

INVESTIGATION

Activity in the Saloon

This saloon building has now become incorporated as part of the hotel, but it has seen a long and varied life since its inception—having been used as a chicken-plucking operation, beauty parlor, mortuary, and general store. The stairs to the upper suites are very tall and shallow, making any ascent a considered journey. They lead to a bedroom with a queen-sized bed tastefully decorated in the style of the 1950s, with cream-colored bedspreads and blue scalloping; across the landing is a small, sage-green-colored sitting room with a matching love seat and rocking chair. I decided to set up a trigger-object experiment on the rocking chair by placing three wooden sticks (from a game of pick-up-sticks) in various strategic places. Halfway through the investigation I came back to discover that two of the sticks were now on the floor—it looked as if somebody had carefully lifted them off the chair and placed them neatly on the ground. I then repeated the experiment with a static video recorder and tripod, in the hope of documenting the incident again—frustratingly, this phenomenon did not reoccur.

A year after the building of the saloon, a schoolhouse was constructed, with the dual purpose of serving as the town hall; this building is now known as the Town House and is believed to be the oldest public-school building in Minnesota. The first teacher was Miss Susan Thompson, who initially taught just four students—but the number rapidly increased as Taylors Falls became a thriving town with a population of over two hundred people. It was officially incorporated in 1858.

Residual Smells in the Old Jail

Despite being surrounded by natural scenic beauty, the darker side of humanity still managed to rear its ugly head; Taylors Falls could be a rough, recidivist community, and a jail was now required to quell lawlessness—as highlighted by the local press:

> A regular "knock down and drag out" row occurred at the Cave saloon last Tuesday night. A boisterous individual from Osceola armed with a revolver, a bowie knife, and a sling shot attempted to "clean out" a party of Swedes who were in the saloon and succeeded in knocking down one or two and cutting another with his knife. He got knocked down and pitched out of the saloon. No arrests were made.[49]

A light anomaly coming through the slats of the staircase from the bedroom was observed by team members and captured by a digital camera

The new jail was placed fortuitously next to the saloon in 1884, with a four-cell building constructed at a cost of $311.76. The cells were created by placing wooden two-by-four planks on top of one another in the hope of making the construction as sturdy as possible; the building was then completed with the addition of a large iron door—which is still visible today. The jail was not as secure as the town would have hoped though, at least according to a one-sentence report from 1881 that tantalizingly fails to explain how an escape was accomplished:

> Two prisoners recently escaped from the jail in Taylors Falls.[50]

Many a libation-infused logger would have been dragged from the saloon to the jail for an overnight stay during its time of operation; on rare occasions, however, the rowdiness was replaced by murder:

> Abe Nelson, who on Christmas Eve killed his aged mother at Taylors Falls by hitting her with a stick of wood, is still confined in the jail for safe keeping. The impression here and at Taylors Falls is that arrangements will be made whereby Nelson's sanity will be tested, and that he will be sent to an insane asylum, his demeanor and action for years before the crime indicating that he is mentally irresponsible.[51]

> Arrested for Murder—Will Parmelee, formerly of Stillwater, is in trouble. He was arrested at Taylors Falls on Tuesday charged with murdering and robbing a saloon-keeper in Iowa about one year ago.[52]

The jail eventually became redundant as other, more modern facilities became available; it was then used for a variety of business ventures, including a garage, shoe-repair shop, and ice-storage facility, and the B & B we see today.

Late one evening a patron made the short journey from the bedroom to the bathroom, only to notice that several mysterious lights had followed her; in a state of pure terror she witnessed the lights manifest themselves into the shapes of a young male child and an old woman. The child appeared to be upset after seeing the fear in the face of the guest and tried to comfort her. "Don't be afraid, miss. We are here to watch over you," he said.

The guest shut her eyes, hoping the manifestations would leave her as quickly as they came; to her relief she opened her eyes and found them to be gone—but sleep was difficult to come by that night.

Getting into the Old Jail to start the first vigil proved to be hazardous in the darkness of a winter's night. The snow and ice on the ground, combined with an uneven path, made me overly cautious with my footing. The first sensation I registered as I entered the building was the cold; I tried to imagine what it must have been like for those imprisoned during the nineteenth century—on a winter's night with no heating and just a bucket for a toilet.

On my immediate right I could see a loft furnished with a queen-sized bed and dresser; farther on I saw a wicker chair in a small alcove and a horse saddle resting on a ledge. The metal stairs led down to the main level, where the living room could be found. The single panes of glass on the windows behind the bars were frosted at the edges, both inside and out, with an icy web that slowly crept into the center of the glass with every passing hour that saw us into the night.

The cold, darkness, and odors must have rendered time to a slow, unbearable crawl during the nineteenth century, dampening the ardor of any raw, ugly moods and tensions that would have been festering within this locked, secure environment. There is now a wood-burning stove to provide warmth to the building with a ready supply of stacked wood—but this was not lit for the investigation. Other comforts now included a soft bed and a claw-footed bathtub. The homey feel of the building was further enhanced through the placement of antique artifacts—ranging from a decorative, dated diving mask to a distressed wooden tea chest.

We had barely begun our vigil when team member Steve R. noticed the chandelier in the kitchen swaying for no reason; there were no drafts present and the team had been sitting motionless—there appeared no clear explanation for this event. Shortly after this incident I noticed a foul stench that was emanating from the rooms surrounding the bathroom; it lasted for several minutes before dissipating and was acknowledged by the other investigators—it was a sulfurous rotting odor. The bathroom was the darkest area of the former jail, as there were no windows in or near the room—it was also in a corner hidden under the stairs. The team mentioned that they all felt an inherent sensation of foreboding in this area, even before the smell arrived. These primeval, internal feelings need to be recognized as important, as these sensations kept us alive during a period of our history when we were prey for long-since-extinct carnivores; this flight-or-fight instinct is an instrument that can perhaps indicate to us the presence of entities that have malicious intentions.

I thought the smell could be a residual odor that had transcended through the centuries—from a time when a toilet bucket existed in a cramped, poorly ventilated cell in the heat of a Minnesota summer. I have smelled perfume, cigar smoke, flowers, and animals on previous investigations, but this was the most offensive smell I have yet encountered. I positioned myself on the second floor near the door; from this vantage point I had a view down the stairs and a sight line into the bedroom. I could also see a good portion of the floor below. I asked if the spirits wanted the bucket removed and emptied, and I then saw a gray-colored orb shoot out through the spindles of the railing near the bed and head towards the door. The light moved from the bedroom in the direction of the bathroom and appeared to be consistent with the stories I had heard. At that moment Lisa saw a shadow figure leave the bathroom. It walked past her, creating a breeze that she felt on her face. All of us then noticed how dark it had become.

I tried to start taking photographs of the bathroom in the hope of capturing the entity, but my camera struggled to find anything to focus on, so would not activate the shutter—a clear indication that the light levels had dropped further (I'd had no problem taking photographs in the same position before the vigil). Then I started to see the shadow myself in the bedroom, between the bed and the spindles of the railings; it appeared to move down the length of the bed and turn back but, tantalizingly, never came out into full view.

When the team had an opportunity to look through the photographs in the evidence review, we saw the usual collection of light anomalies caused by dust particles and water vapor; an exception to this would be a photograph Angela had taken looking down the stairs—in which you can clearly see what looks like a small, solid, and white tube-shaped object on the stairs. This was the light anomaly the team had seen darting through the building.

Towards the end of the vigil I decided to use the ghost box. The town's predominantly Swedish heritage led me to try and tease a dialogue out by using some basic Swedish words and phrases. This included saying hello, and asking if they spoke English and what their name was—Hej. *Talar du engelska? Vad heter du?*

Disappointingly, this produced no significant results. As I concluded the vigil, a loud groan was heard coming from the opposite end of the building. Several members of the investigation team heard this sound, but unfortunately it failed to be audible on our DVRs as the ghost box was still running and obliterated the recorded sound.

At the end of the vigil I asked Don, the owner, if he had noticed the foul odor before. He had never encountered anything like that in the building previously and informed me that all the pipe work was in good working order and in continuous use. Discussions with Don and Kate have subsequently revealed that this phenomenon has not been repeated.

Sensitives can acquire psychic knowledge by means of smell; this is often referred to as *clairolfaction, clairescence,* or *clairalience*—which literally means "clear-smelling." This instance was not a psychic phenomenon though; it was physically present (as much as a smell can be). Those who have witnessed paranormal activity often recall the smell of sulfur as being part of their experience; this would be true of many paranormal encounters throughout history. Lightning or energy is also often reported to be accompanied by sulfurous smells, so it is no surprise that the two are complementary to one another in mythology when describing the retribution of gods.

The link between big discharges of lightning energy combined with foul-smelling sulfur was documented in biblical times, when the judgment of the Lord was linked to fire and brimstone—during the destruction of Sodom and Gomorrah, for example. Historical Greek literature also links sulfur with deity activity, as described in Homer's twelfth book of the *Odyssey*:

> Zeus thundered and hurled his bolt upon the ship and she quivered from stem to stern, smitten by the bolt of Zeus, and was filled with sulfurous smoke.[53]

Homer continues this theme in the *Iliad*:

> [Zeus] thundered horribly and dashed it to the ground in front of the horses of Diomedes, and a ghastly blaze of flaming sulfur shot up and the horses, terrified, both cringed away against the chariot.[54]

Benjamin Franklin's first experiments with lightning led him to describe a sulfurous smell in the notes he forwarded to the Royal Society in London. Much later, it was scientifically suggested by Russian-born scholar Immanuel Velikovsky (1895–1979) that sulfur could be generated when an electrical discharge was passed through air—although he theorized that an enormous amount of energy would be required for oxygen to be transmuted into sulfur.

It is believed that entities also require energy to be physical or to manifest themselves—this can be witnessed as light anomalies or as a glowing form (as photographed during our vigil in the Old Jail). It would then be reasonable to believe that energy passing through the air could create the sulfurous smells we encountered at the Old Jail; this could also provide an explanation for the match smells in the saloon. It makes me consider that sulfur smells could travel through a window created between two dimensions when an entity enters our own time; such an event could inform previous encounters with similar smells during periods of high activity—as in the Palmer House basement, for example.

CONCLUSION

The small town of Taylors Falls was actually one of the most talked-about locations in the world during the year 1886; that June a monumental logjam was the subject of articles in newspapers around the globe. This was believed to be the worst logjam in recorded history—it was estimated that 150 million logs were congested into a three-mile stretch of the river. Smaller logjams were not uncommon in this area, and perhaps experiences during the summer of 1878 should have provided an insight into the disaster that was to follow several years later:

> The big jam at Taylors Falls commences at the Dalles, near the bridge, and runs back to Thompson's flouring mill. There are now 20,000,000 in it, and the logs are rapidly running in. River men think it will take some time to break the jam, but as yet there is nothing definite.[55]

Sightseers would pay to see the logjams via the river, and a lucrative business boomed for anyone in possession of a steamship:

> Excursions today to see the great jam of logs at the Dalles of the St. Croix on the steamer G. B. *Knapp*. Boat leaves at St. Paul, Stillwater & Taylors Falls railroad depot at 8 o'clock a.m. F. E. Joy, manager.[56]

By 1880 observers could travel from St. Paul on the railroad, allowing people to view the glacial-carved landscapes and Swiss-inspired architecture. Six years later, over one thousand tourists per day took advantage of this to marvel at the logjam. Dynamite was initially used to try and break up the logjam with the aid of steamships and tow ropes, but this proved unsuccessful; a team of 175 men was then employed to work around the clock under makeshift lights to try and release the jam by hand, something that took them over six weeks to achieve. Unfortunately, this came too late for many of the mills farther downstream, which subsequently went out of business.

The investigation at the Old Jail and Saloon gave me the paranormal first of experiencing such a prominent and significant smell (unlike any other paranormal smells I had previously come across). I was disappointed that contact was not made with Etta or the steamship captain, but spirits very rarely do anything on command. I was pleased to link the sulfur-match smell with the death of baby Frank, and the light anomalies and shadow figures I witnessed in the Old Jail were very intriguing. More evidence will be recorded on further visits to the Old Jail, and slowly more of the paranormal puzzle will come together.

CHAPTER 12

The St. James Hotel

RED WING

The ghost of a previous owner, a terrifying floating phantom head, and the mischievous haunting of the guest rooms make the St. James Hotel a retreat full of paranormal activity.

The St. James Hotel in Red Wing, Goodhue County, was the site of a weekend-long investigation undertaken with the biggest team I have yet assembled. The manager was happy for us to explore the entire building and was very accommodating. I asked to investigate the hotel after hearing stories about the alleged hauntings that were taking place there (including a ghostly phantom floating head and the spirit of a woman named Clara Nelson). My research was undertaken at the Minnesota Historical Society through period newspapers and the various documents that detailed much of the Native American activity on the land. The staff and management of the hotel also provided extensive historical information, literature, and photographs.

HISTORY

Red Wing's location on the banks of the Mississippi River was recognized as ideal for steamship access from the first moment a vessel moored itself there in May 1823; it was called the *Virginia* and was navigating its way from St. Louis to the newly constructed Fort Snelling. Chief Hupahuduta and several other prominent local Native Americans were invited onboard to meet the crew and passengers. They sat and smoked a peace pipe and engaged in conversation (although it is impossible to ascertain how much each party understood of the other). Red Wing was incorporated as a city in 1857, and by the 1870s a rapid development of the docking facilities and trading port allowed it to become the world's largest supplier of wheat (its dockside warehouses boasted the storage capacity of one million bushels).

The spread of the railroads started to diminish this method of wheat distribution, as river transportation was overtaken by the quicker and more economical locomotives. Subsequently, industrial development replaced more agricultural endeavors and saw added wealth and commerce come into Red Wing. The continued success of the area brought with it an increase in businessmen and traders, and there was also a newly found boom in tourism, as the scenic Mississippi River Valley became accessible through the railroad—enabling visitors from farther afield to experience the views and to participate in the pursuits of walking and climbing. The local limestone formations that once provided

The St. James Hotel, Red Wing

The St. James Hotel circa 1875

the raw materials to build Red Wing were now providing a challenge for hikers.

A modern, spacious, and first-class lodging establishment was required to satisfy the need created by these new demands. Eleven like-minded, civic-thinking businessmen created the Red Wing Hotel Corporation and began to raise funds to finance the building of a hotel—$60,000 was raised through a joint-stock company venture of local citizens, and construction was started in the spring of 1874. Their achievements are remembered for posterity in the fading sepia photographs of the eleven entrepreneurs that line the grand staircase—the original document listing their individual contributions is framed and hangs resplendently in the library.

NATIVE AMERICAN BODIES IN THE BASEMENT

It could be argued that fate was playing a hand in disrupting the building of the hotel; initially, construction had to stop after unseasonably high summer temperatures made it impossible for laborers to work. Then a stark reminder of Red Wing's past was uncovered, when two skeletal remains were unearthed as foundations were dug, into what was believed to be an ancient Native American burial ground. This desecration of Native American remains from deep within the heart of the hotel could be the catalyst for much of the paranormal activity that is intrinsic to the fabric of the building. Despite these setbacks, the hotel was completed and opened during the following year.

The earliest people to live in the area of Red Wing were the Mdewakanton Dakota tribe—they were a sub-tribe of the Isanti Dakota (Santee Sioux). Their ancestors had made the long and hazardous migration into present-day Wisconsin via Ohio, before traveling farther west to Minnesota. They called their new settlement by the Mississippi River *Proymueche*, which translates as "mountain in the water," or *Hemminnicha*, which combines the words, *wood, water, and hill*.

The first documented visit of a white man in Red Wing occurred when the explorer and priest Father Louis Hennepin arrived in April 1680. The Mdewakanton were always very friendly and welcomed the gradual trickle of white men who passed through their land. The majority of what is now the Midwest west of the Mississippi River was under Spanish and then French control during this period—until 1803, when the United States bought the land under the Louisiana Purchase.

With the area now under American ownership, Colonel Zebulon Pike of the U.S. Army journeyed to the site in September 1805, in order to survey the area and to hold a meeting with Chief Hupahuduta (whose name can be translated as "dyed red swan's wing"—which he carried around with him as a symbol of his leadership). It was on June 30, 1823, that Red Wing was first placed on the map, when Major Stephen Long paid a visit to the settlement and raised the Stars and Stripes above the Indian council house for the first time. Long suggested that the settlement be renamed Red Wing.

By 1837 the Mdewakanton were finding themselves under increasing pressure by the Ojibwe and other local Native Americans to remove themselves from Wisconsin and to stay within the boundaries of Minnesota—ecological circumstances also persuaded the Mdewakanton people to continue their diaspora westward. Pressure was then applied from the U.S. government, which wanted them to sign a removal treaty to relinquish western Wisconsin. They reluctantly agreed to give up their claim to the land:

> The chiefs and head men of the Mdewakanton Sioux were taken to Washington, where, by a treaty, confirmed by the Senate in the succeeding year, in consideration of $991,000, they ceded to the United States a vast tract of country, including this spot. The

words of cession are so brief that they could be written between the blowing out of a candle and its ignition again from the fire left in the wick. Here they are: The chiefs and braves representing the parties having an interest herein cede to the United States all their lands east of the Mississippi River and all their islands in the said river.[57]

Within fifteen minutes and with thirty-two words, the Mdewakanton had lost a vast swath of their land. The Mdewakanton would never be paid the full amount, however, and much of the money was offset against the cost of forcibly educating the tribe through programs designed to bring "civilization" to them.

The next treaty that had a direct impact on Red Wing was agreed to on July 29, 1851, in Mendota—this allowed white settlers to make their homes on the banks of the river from 1853 onwards. John Day became the first pioneer in 1852 to leave his home in Trenton, Wisconsin, cross the Mississippi, and stake a claim to the land. He sheltered in the former missionary building while erecting a log cabin nearby; the Mdewakanton were obviously unhappy with the outcome of the treaty because they immediately destroyed the cabin. Day proceeded to rebuild the cabin a further six times—with it being destroyed on each occasion. Day then decided to wait until the following year when the treaty would come into full effect.

The geographical advantages of Red Wing, with its fertile prairie next to the river and bluffs and its abundance of natural resources and river trade, saw a flood of immigrant pioneers push the Mdewakanton away to areas farther north and west.

INVESTIGATION

The Phantom Floating Head

The basement of the hotel was the most obvious starting point for the investigation; you can touch the cold walls of the foundations and believe that just feet from your fingertips lie the remains of bodies—possibly surrounding you in their hundreds. Kitchen workers in the basement regularly claim to witness the horrific sight of ghostly faces and heads coming out of the darkness at them—with cold, dead, hollow eyes that stare in accusation. They also report a feeling of uneasiness and the sense of a strong male dominance in this vicinity, with the common phenomenon of catching a movement out of the corner of their eyes—only to discover that they are on their own.

One would like to believe that the bodies unearthed in 1874 were dealt with in a dignified and proper manner—but there are no records to clarify this. It could be suggested that these ancient fractured remains may have been cleared from the site without all of their skeletal parts fully retrieved. It is possible that an unfound skull could provide the explanation for the existence of a disembodied head roaming the basement—perhaps looking to be reunited with its body. Certainly a decapitation could also be considered, as Native Americans, frontiersmen, settlers, and U.S. government troops all participated in this practice. Rewards for scalps and heads were first introduced amongst the British authorities in America during Dummer's War of 1722–25, when a bounty of a hundred pounds was offered for each one presented—expeditions were organized solely for the capture of these grisly trophies. Other examples of this practice can be seen in the actions of the government of Massachusetts in 1744, the French colonists in 1749, and the settlers of Halifax during the same year.

Bloody fighting with edged weapons between the Mdewakanton and rival tribes was also an ongoing situation that could result in the loss of a head. In 1807 Chief Shakea of the Mdewakanton was on a hunting trip when he dreamt his tribe was being attacked—this turned out to be a premonition. The following night the Ojibwe attacked the encampment, killing several of the Mdewakanton before they could muster a counterattack, and forcing the Ojibwe to retreat. The Mdewakanton then succeeded in getting ahead of the Ojibwe and surrounded them on a wooded river island—many Ojibwe were massacred.

Fighting between the white settlers and the Mdewakanton would also have contributed to this kind of death. During the Dakota War of 1862, the normally peaceful Mdewakanton were driven to bloody conflict; a later newspaper article outlines the attack on the Redwood Agency in southwestern Minnesota:

> On Monday, the 18th, about 8 o'clock a.m. word came to the upper agency at Yellow Medicine that all the white people at the Lower, or Redwood agency, had been murdered by the Mdewakanton Sioux—the Mdewakanton had already gone so far that the worst that the whites could inflict would be sure to come among them all—that the whites would regard them

all alike as enemies, and, since matters could in no event be worse, the best plan was to kill them all and take their goods.[58]

During these Sioux attacks a convention developed for scalping and beheading, as highlighted in this article from the Sauk Centre Herald in 1871:

Skull Found.—On Thursday, Mr. L. B. Raymond brought to town a human skull which was picked up by his son in the town of Ashley about five miles south east of this place [Sauk Centre]. It is supposed to be the head of Mr. T. Van Eaton, who nine years ago, during the Indian Massacre, after having brought his family from Grove Lake to the stockade, at this place, went back next day to get his cattle and was killed by the Indians. The body was found except the head, which had been cut off. There is very little doubt that the skull found by young Raymond is the missing portion of Mr. Van Eaton's body, having been carried a few miles by the Indians and thrown down, where it has lain bleached for nine years.[59]

Incidents like this fostered copycat reprisals, and Native American burial sites could have seen warriors laid to rest with their heads detached from their bodies—or with no heads at all.

After the vigil I moved from the lower-level basement and kitchen to the banquet area, where I met Kate from the second team near the entrance to the larger of the two rooms. I could tell straightaway by her pallid face that she had seen something paranormal; she was quivering and trying to regain her composure—as her teeth chattered together in shock. She exclaimed that she had seen a floating head at the far end of the longer banquet room. She rushed me to the spot where she had witnessed the apparition and pointed towards the exit doors. "There," she said. "It was floating in the dark with two large yellow eyes!"

She described the head coming towards her out of the darkness (just as the staff had documented). I asked her if there were any other details she could recall; she described the head as male with long, dark, straggly hair and with eyes that did not appear to have pupils. I did not want to put the suggestion into Kate's head, but I had to ask whether she thought the head looked Native American; she replied that it did. We swept the area with thermometers and EMF meters but recorded no unusual data.

Spooky World

Other suggested paranormal activity in the basement is documented through the sounds of voices and talking, but this could easily be attributed to the location of the Port of Red Wing restaurant next door, creating the possibility of voices being heard from external sources. It is also reported that objects move and rattle on their own in the basement kitchen and storage areas—utensils, pots, pans, wine bottles, and dishes sway with such regularity that the furthest storage rooms have been christened "Spooky World" by the employees. It could be argued though that the regularity with which heavy trucks pass by on the highway directly outside the hotel could account for the gentle swaying of the hanging kitchenalia that jostles, clinks, and kisses together under the metronomic vibration. Further events that evening, however, would be less easy to explain away.

The Ghostly Breathing

From the main lobby the investigation team went through the back corner door and descended into the stairwell, which eventually led to a room buried deep within the lowest part of the basement. This maintenance area has a metal-mesh security door that reminded me of a cage. Several members of staff told me that a person had died down there—but I found no proof to back up these claims (it could be true, but I have no documentation to support their statements).

It is good practice when taking photographs during a vigil to preface any shot with the word "Flash," so that other investigators have a chance to turn away or close their eyes. If you look inadvertently at a camera flash in the dark, you will be left seeing light anomalies for the rest of the evening. From the audio recordings of the vigil you can clearly hear a man's voice repeating my words back to me, so when I say "Flash," a second voice says, "Flash" directly after me. It responded to other words throughout this session, too—as I counted down to taking a photograph by saying, "One ... two ... three," it said, "Go," and then uttered the phrase "Do it," after I said, "Let me try something."

Just before we closed the vigil in the basement, Warren stated that he felt the sensation of breath upon his neck; in the dim light of the equipment I could see the hairs on the back of his neck standing up. At that point Warren exclaimed that a dark shadow had dropped down in front of him, to almost confront him (he could not make out any facial features though).

It did appear that the darkness was more pronounced around Warren than in any other part of the room. I told him to move around, and the darkness seemed to follow him. At one point a chair moved by itself next to where he was walking, making a discernible noise.

The Architecture

On top of the foundations a five-story hotel in the Romanesque Italian style was built; it was designed by the St. Paul-based architect Edward Payson Bassford (1837–1912). Bassford was a well-respected architect born in Calais, Maine. He studied in Boston before enlisting in Company B of the 44th Massachusetts Regiment at the beginning of the Civil War. After the conflict he got married and moved to St. Paul to set up his business. He was a highly regarded architect, and the Red Wing Hotel Corporation was fortunate to procure his services; his portfolio included the St. Paul courthouse and city hall, the Guardian Building, the McColl Building, the William Catzson House, and the Nicollet County courthouse and jail. He also oversaw the construction of the federal courthouse in St. Paul (now the Landmark Center).

The hotel was officially opened on Thanksgiving Day in 1875. Five hundred lucky ticket holders paid five dollars each to celebrate and explore the hotel. They marveled at the mix of traditional, plush furnishings and experienced the expensively extravagant patterned Brussels carpet, which welcomed the weary feet of travelers into the lobby before guiding them into the beautiful dining rooms. The working function of the hotel was carefully considered by Bassford; a hotel office, a baggage-storage area, and a state-of-the-art kitchen were all part of the building's design. The lower level reflected the male domination of this era with a barbershop, billiard hall, parlor, public baths, and gentlemen's water closets. Ladies were not without their comforts though, and a deep, soft, voluptuous English velvet carpet spread itself into the ladies' parlor on the second floor. This level also featured two ladies' water closets and a bridal suite.

For those not distracted by the first four levels, the sight of an elegant ballroom on the fifth floor awaited those who achieved ascension to the top, with stained-glass-lined hallways and art-adorned ceilings. Such visitors would also be rewarded with views of the river and Red Wing from the large floor-to-ceiling windows on each side. All of these features were combined with the modernity of gas fittings, a steam-heating system on every floor, and running hot water; for those with enough capital, a harsh Minnesota winter in the 1870s could almost be bearable.

The St. James Hotel in many ways reflects the very essence of what pioneering America was: it is an Italian-styled building with European features that successfully mixes elements of the old with the new, built democratically by committee on Native American land and opened on Thanksgiving Day. Given the keys on that celebratory morning (and employed with the honor of running this magnificent new hotel) were two brothers: E. A. and F. A. Blood, from Oshkosh, Wisconsin.

Not surprisingly, the hotel was an immediate success and quickly became the hub of the entire town; it was booked to capacity every night as patrons streamed steadily from the train station and steamships to sample the hospitality and the food. The hotel's reputation for culinary delights began to be recognized nationally; even President Rutherford B. Hayes dined at the hotel. Uniquely, the railroad company actually changed its timetables so patrons could disembark in time for dinner. The Blood brothers finally passed along the keys in 1909, after thirty-four highly successful years, to new owner Charles Lillyblad.

The Ghost of Clara

Romance was always prevalent within the hotel's ornate surroundings and décor—with newlywed couples enjoying their first night together in the luxurious suites and surroundings. Cupid's arrow did not discriminate though, when in 1914 the new owner saw Clara Nelson for the first time across the busy dining room as she waited on tables. Charles and Clara were soon married, and Clara embraced the role of the owner's wife by increasing the hotel's culinary reputation further with her forward-thinking ideas for sourcing the freshest and highest-quality local produce to use in her recipes. Her home-cooked meats and pies became legendary, and her dining area was soon referred to by the locals as "Clara's Place."

The more I discovered about Clara during my research, the more I believed that her spirit could still be present in the hotel; she was meticulous in her attention to detail and demanded the highest standards from her staff. She oversaw every aspect of the hotel from top to bottom—from the unseen maintenance and pot-washing to the more visible sparkling tableware and cutlery of the front-of-house hospitality. This attention to detail, combined with her assiduity towards every aspect of running the hotel, would lead me

The spirit of Clara Lillyblad is said to reside in the hotel

to believe that she would be reluctant to relinquish her hold over the building—even after her passing.

Her nature was also very generous; she would go out of her way to help those down on their luck or with difficulties concerning money. She always opened her kitchen on Christmas Day to provide a free dinner (with all the trimmings) for those who asked if food was available. Clara also made sure during the festive period that recently widowed Red Wing citizens were given a turkey courtesy of the hotel. Nor were the staff forgotten; they were treated every year to a full Christmas party, with food, drinks, and presents. On one occasion she famously allowed a poor, rural newlywed couple to dine in luxury for the cost of the cheapest meal on the menu—as all their savings had been spent on their room for the night.

This nurturing aspect of Clara's character would certainly suggest she would hang around to make sure people were comfortable and had everything they needed to make their stay a happy one. Charles Lillyblad died in 1932, but Clara continued to run the hotel with her son, Art; he was born in 1916 in Room 208 and started helping out in the hotel at the tender age of seven. Clara died in 1972, and Art continued to run the hotel until 1977; astonishingly, the St. James Hotel was owned by only two families in 102 years.

The hotel was then purchased by the Red Wing Shoe Company and underwent a two-year, multimillion dollar restoration project; it was refitted extensively and reopened for business in July 1979. Part of the redevelopment incorporated a refurbishment of rooms 310 and 311. They are both situated at the end of a long hallway in the historic part of the hotel and were originally occupied by Clara and her family—this would be the location of the next vigil.

Room 310

I became instantly aware of how cold it was when I first walked into Room 310—my portable thermometer showed a reading of 57.5 degrees Fahrenheit. I attributed the low room temperature to the hotel's energy-saving policy for unoccupied rooms and the rapidly falling Minnesota winter night temperatures. The décor was resplendent, with high pressed ceilings, handcarved woodwork, bronze features, floral print wallpaper, a dresser bureau, and a beautiful dark, wood-framed mirror—which reflected a dominating high four-poster bed complete with a pristine white bedspread. Many of the original light fixtures are still in use, and as I placed my finger on the switch to plunge the room into darkness, I imagined Clara repeating the same action a thousand times before me in the past.

Paranormal activity in this part of the hotel has added to the legend of Clara—she has been seen as a full-bodied apparition moving around these rooms. During our vigil the team sensed that someone was standing and observing us from the left-hand corner of the room next to the night stand. As we tried to process this sensation, Steve R. called out, "In the mirror! I saw something there!"

This was followed by Kate exclaiming, "I saw it, too!"

What they had witnessed was a quick movement of some kind reflected in the farthest right-hand side of the mirror. This motion was too quick to decipher, but it could be described as a shadow of some sort; it was intriguing that several members of the team saw the same movement.

Paranormal Energy in the Dining Room

The lobby leads into a Victorian dining room, and Clara is said to still be in control of this area. Many other hotels I have investigated still have dead, dominating previous owners that want to interfere with the day-to-day running of the business. There is the sensation of being watched in this area, too, and this fits well with the idea that Clara is overseeing her staff and wanting to supervise. There is a large, heavy, round wooden table in this room; this table was crafted and built with pride, and the shiny patina visibly shows the history of well over a century of serving meals. It is claimed that a resistance pushes

The Victorian dining room and Clara's table

against anyone who tries to move the table away from its current position, as if an unseen force is stopping the table from being maneuvered into a different area.

Kate pulled up a chair and sat at the table; the very second she sat down and placed her hands upon the wooden table surface, the K2 EMF meter (which was placed in the middle of the table) spiked into the red with a reading of over 25 milligauss. When Kate removed her hands from the table the meter fell back down to its neutral baseline reading; this process continued every time her hands were placed on the table and removed again.

Was it possible Clara was present with us and was reacting in an uptight manner whenever it looked as if the table might be moved? The timing and duration of the lights illuminating in sequence with Kate's actions could certainly suggest it was. I noted the temperature of the table at the beginning of this session at 68.3 degrees Fahrenheit. The reading at the end of the experiment was 66.3 degrees Fahrenheit—not a great drop in temperature but significant enough to question why it had become colder during such a short period of time; no natural explanation could be found for this.

We proceeded to undertake a series of EVP sweeps to see if further contact could be made, but the sensitivity of our audio equipment managed only to record the noise contamination coming from the mechanical process of the heating system, which could easily be misinterpreted as distant whispers. The nature of investigating in a working hotel will always provide us with strange, extraneous noises, which could just be a guest treading on a squeaky floorboard above us as he accesses a glass of water.

We used the ghost box towards the end of the vigil with little success until I declared we were going to leave; the ghost box then said, "We're leaving"—and at that point Lisa felt a cold breeze brush against her body. I asked if they would like to follow us to the next area, and the ghost box replied, "No"—which was definitive.

Power Drain in the Lobby

The lobby is dominated by an enormous wooden check-in desk. At night the whole area is intermittently lit by passing traffic. Traces of light race across the walls and ceiling accompanied by faint, randomly occurring rumbles—which are fused with the locomotion and distant voices of pedestrians. Leading off from the lobby I glimpsed the photographic portraits that run the length of the grand stairwell, belonging to long-since-dead benefactors. As their eyes became illuminated by the transient traffic I could easily imagine my mind being tricked into the sensation of being watched.

I continued into a room with an ornate, beautifully styled German pipe organ and a baby grand piano—all framed by a high, pressed-tin ceiling supported by fluted columns. Well-dressed ladies and gentlemen would have stood around in their evening clothes, waiting to enter the Victorian dining room for their dinner; the men would have congregated to the small lounge in front of the cozy open fire for a pre-prandial drink and then withdrawn here with brandy, cigars, and full stomachs.

The original lobby entrance still exists, allowing us to experience the first impressions guests had back in 1875, when they pushed themselves through the etched-glass doors into a sea of sheer opulence and grandeur. However, the earliest guests would not have experienced what I discovered as I entered the hotel—which was a battery drain on all my equipment; the hotel was very vampiric on batteries. I had to replace them in my DVR three times, and my newly charged digital-camera batteries went flat almost immediately—this can normally be attributed to very cold and damp investigation conditions, but the hotel lobby did not fall into this category. It is believed that spirits are capable of taking and using the energy sources you have in your equipment in order to help them to manifest or be physical.

The Haunted Third Floor

It is true to say that paranormal activity tends to be stimulated by renovation and construction work—this was true for the third-floor offices; activity in this area only began when building work started. Several reasons may exist to explain this phenomenon; it is possible that the physicality and noise of the construction work may have stirred or woken a lost memory that has imprinted a residual haunting onto a space—or jolts a spirit back into activity. A residual haunting may have always been there but became more noticeable (especially if it was hidden by furniture or walls) after the construction work began. It could also disturb an entity that was attached to an object—like a favorite chair, for example, that has been moved or engaged with in some way, or a portrait that has been taken down to enable a wall to be painted or papered.

It is also recognized that activity may be a sign to show us a previous owner or employee is unhappy with changes that are currently taking place. I am sure if Clara were unhappy with the way the hotel was being developed, she would make her opinion and her annoyance known—a critique on interior design from beyond the grave.

The image of a small girl in an old, period-style, white dress is seen running through this office from wall to wall—this activity only started when the construction work began, and the frequency of this sighting increased as the building work continued. She has only been seen between the hours of five a.m. and seven a.m. though—which suggests the haunting is residual in nature.

It is reasonable to assume that before this room was an office, it was a bedroom; the child who occupied it could have been the daughter of one of the staff or a family member. Her happy, playful nature appears to have been captured for those lucky enough to be present in the early hours of the morning—it is worth noting that ghostly sightings are not always about unhappy or traumatic events. Evidence does suggest that this room develops cold spots in the locations where the girl appears and disappears.

The Spirit in Room 414

I was given Room 414 for the duration of my stay. All of the rooms are named after the steamships that once navigated Red Wing via the Mississippi (414 was called *Wakerobin*). As I ventured in, passing the expanse of a king-sized bed, I found myself surrounded by oversized, rich, dark-wood fixtures and elaborate decorated fabrics and furnishings in beautiful hues of blue. Despite its homey feel, I experienced a sensation of foreboding as I stepped into the space. The atmosphere felt heavy and oppressive, and my body erupted in goose bumps. Before going to bed I made a mental note of the room's layout, paying careful attention to where the furniture and decorative objects were placed—I expected paranormal activity to be prevalent that night.

When I awoke the following morning I discovered the door to the armoire wide open—when I know it had been shut tight the previous night. I inspected the armoire and noted that it was tipped back at a slight angle; this would have stopped the door coming open of its own accord. I tried to re-create the action of the door opening by itself, but found this to be impossible—unless I physically opened the door with my hand. When I left the room briefly that morning I placed my watch on the nightstand next to the bed, but when I returned an hour later the watch had vanished. I rediscovered it lying on top of the desk at the opposite side of the room. I checked with the staff to find out if any housekeeping had taken place during my absence—it had not. These incidents prompted me to organize an extra vigil to see what we could ascertain here.

We started our vigil in Room 414 with the ghost box; within minutes of beginning, several different voices came through that said the same word over and over—the word was *dead*. In a short spell we counted the word *dead* being said another twenty times—this was then followed by the phrase "Please help me."

We asked what help they needed, but additional communication was not forthcoming. It was a great frustration that we could not gain further insight into the distressing nature of these statements; perhaps they were afraid to talk further or were simply being stopped by other forces.

CONCLUSION

The St. James Hotel could be compared to a maze—meandering, twisting, and turning with long hallways and stairs that to the unfamiliar would appear to lead nowhere; you could easily spend a year paranormally investigating the building, and you would still not have accessed every area. I suspect the number of spirits residing here or passing through on any given day to be very high.

Relationships and trust are built up with spirits over a prolonged period, like any other relationship, and they will remember the team. It is interesting to note that I have been asked for in other locations I regularly investigate, by spirits talking to other teams, wondering where I am. I shall keep coming back to the St. James Hotel; and I shall keep asking questions; and I will keep offering my services—one day the spirits may tell me why they need help. Let's hope when that day comes, I can provide it.

CHAPTER 13

Schmidt Brewery

ST. PAUL

Kidnapping, gangland activities, and industrial accidents mean the only thing now brewing in this disused factory is paranormal activity.

The Schmidt Brewery is a very impressive building and is a recognizable feature of the St. Paul skyline. I had often driven past its splendid façade and wondered if it was haunted. I took the team into the location over a single night and explored the many intricate facets of its interior. The Minnesota Historical Society in St. Paul had a thick folder of documents and archive materials that gave me a thorough insight into the brewery; high-profile historical incidents also allowed me to uncover period newspaper articles, both at the historical society and online.

HISTORY

In 1855 beer production was started by the Cave Brewery on the site of the Schmidt Brewery—three years before Minnesota gained statehood. Brewers saw the benefits of using the naturally occurring underground water for the beer-making process and started filling the air around St. Paul with the distinctive aroma of yeast and hops—a smell that was to be a familiar constant for the next 147 years. Its location on West 7th Street evolved from humble beginnings into the hub of a thriving German brewing culture with a fifteen-acre site and a factory floor covering over 100,000 square feet. By 1879 the factory had been renamed the Stahlmann Brewing Company and became the first Minnesota brewery to sell more than 10,000 barrels a year—exporting its wares as far south as Tennessee.

The brewery gained the famous name of Schmidt at the beginning of the twentieth century. Jacob Schmidt was born in Bavaria on October 9, 1845, and like many German immigrants, arrived in the United States via New York—when he was just twenty years old. From 1840 to 1880, German immigrants made up the largest group of foreign nationals entering America. This was primarily due to the 1848 revolutions in the German states and the wave of political upheaval that followed, creating a flood of political refugees.

The birth of the brewing industry in Minnesota coincided with this influx; the contemporary knowledge the Germans brought with them of the brewing process was to prove invaluable across the Midwest. This included introducing the new technique of "lagering"—in which fermentation was facilitated at the bottom of the vat rather than at the top. This was achieved over a longer duration and with an added refrigerated

The Schmidt Brewery after our investigation, as the sun came up

The Schmidt Brewery, circa 1910

storage period of several months (*Lager* means "storage" in German); this would have taken place in the coldness of the caves.

Jacob started to share his brewing education in Milwaukee and New York, before coming to St. Paul to assist his friend Theodore Hamm in the position of brewmaster at the Hamm's brewery. He then gained more experience by traveling to New Ulm to work at the Schell's Brewery and several other breweries throughout the Midwest. By 1884 Jacob had moved back to St. Paul and went into joint ownership of the North Star Brewery, located at Commercial Street and Hudson Road. It was during this period that the strange series of events that seemed to follow the Schmidt family around started to occur.

RANDOM SHOOTING

A string of bizarre events may have left a layer of negative energy over the entire location; sometimes it is difficult to ascertain whether these incidents add to the energy or are caused by the energy. On July 4, 1893, two men arrived at the bank behind the brewery on a boat and proceeded to start shooting pigeons. A man matching Jacob's description appeared on the roof of the brewery and discharged a rifle five times at the two men; one of the men was hit in the left breast as the bullet penetrated under his arm. The two men managed to fashion an escape back onto the boat before contacting the police. The men told a police officer that the culprit was Jacob Schmidt and that he was wearing a pink shirt and a flop hat. When Jacob Schmidt was apprehended, he was indeed wearing a pink shirt and a flop hat; he was brought into custody. The *Saint Paul Daily Globe* reported on the injured man's condition:

> Theodore Beaudoin, who was shot, July 4 while near Schmidt's brewery, is reported much improved and on the road to recovery. Jacob Schmidt, who, it is claimed did the shooting, will have an examination on that charge in the police court on Saturday.[60]

Jacob was taken to the Ducas Street police station and held in custody until bail was arranged. Theodore spent the next fourteen days in the hospital and was lucky not to lose his life; the bullet had miraculously managed to miss his vital organs. Jacob was actually able to provide an alibi for the incident: he claimed he was engaging in a card game in his office at the time of the shooting with a number of his close friends. Subsequently, Jacob was released without charge.

Jacob retired by 1899 and turned his business operations over to his daughter Mary and his son-in-law Adolph Bremer. Jacob originally hired the much younger Adolph to be his bookkeeper—he was also a German immigrant with knowledge of the brewing industry. They immediately started a lifelong friendship that culminated with Adolph becoming a member of the Schmidt family when he married Jacob's daughter Mary in 1896. Adolph went on to become the vice president of the company, with his brother Otto Bremer occupying the position of company secretary and treasurer. Otto was very experienced; he was the president of the American National Bank and served for more than a decade as the treasurer of the city of St. Paul. In later years he became an advisor to U.S. presidents Woodrow Wilson and Franklin D. Roosevelt, the latter of whom appointed Otto to manage the Federal Home Owner's Loan Corporation of Minnesota.

At this time the brewery was a relatively small family business with only twelve employees, but the transition to Mary and Adolph was not without its difficulties. Barely a year had passed when the brewery burned to the ground. Everything was destroyed, and a new location was quickly required. The Jacob Schmidt Brewing Company incorporated itself into the current location in 1901, and the Bremers instantly went about constructing a new plant and malt house next to the existing structures. This was the beginning of a building program that was to make the Schmidt Brewery one of the most distinguishing landmarks of St. Paul.

THE ARCHITECTURE

What the stunning architectural splendor of the brewery captures is the dramatic technological and commercial evolution of the brewing industry over several centuries, from the 1880 stone malt houses to the 1949 grain elevator. The primary architect Bernard Barthel had the difficult task of integrating the requirements of height and the formal complexities of the brewing process into his plans, creating a building that represents form and function in equal measure.

The medieval towers and turrets with their neoclassical features and cobblestone streets conjure a romantic and eye-catching expression of European architectural vernacular—reminiscent of a picturesque castle perched on the banks of the Rhine. The ornamental cornices and denticulate modillions are all perfectly formed in Bedford stone trim; the checkered voussoir pattern of the window arches in tan and cream-colored bricks highlight the grandeur and empirical might of the Schmidt brewing dynasty. Jacob Schmidt died on September 2, 1910, so he never got to witness how this landmark film set of a building was to evolve so spectacularly.

THE KIDNAPPING

This visually impressive building was also the backdrop to more dark energy—laced with kidnapping, organized crime, and Prohibition. On January 17, 1934, Edward G. Bremer (the son of Mary and Adolph Bremer) was kidnapped; this was a crime that would spark the nation's imagination, and it is now placed firmly in the canon of American criminology. Bremer was the president of the Commercial State Bank of St. Paul. When he left for work that morning with his daughter Betty he could not have imagined that he would be on the front page of every national newspaper by the following morning; after dropping off Betty at her private school, he continued his journey to work.

His clockwork regularity saw him stop at the same intersection at the same time every day; on this particular day Bremer was shocked to find several armed men jumping into his black Lincoln sedan. With the cold, gray gun metal pressed against his trembling temple, he was ordered to drive! He followed the men's directions, his mind racing with all the possible outcomes of how this scenario could end—not one of them good.

He was forced to pull over in an isolated spot, and the blow of a blunt, hard object rendered him unconscious—the gang did not want to give away the location of their hideout. They continued their journey for almost four hundred miles, to a house in Bensenville, Illinois. The gang was well known to the FBI as the Barker–Karpis gang, named after Alvin Karpis and Freddie Barker—assisted by Arthur "Doc" Barker, Volger Davis, and Harry Campbell. This gang was probably better known, though, as the Ma Barker Gang.

There was friction within the gang about the idea of venturing away from bank robberies into the overly complicated area of kidnapping. Karpis had misgivings about taking Edward Bremer, due to his family's alleged underworld connections in Chicago, forged during Prohibition (the ability to brew alcohol was a useful tool in that era). Unfortunately for them, the gang was unaware (or chose not to acknowledge) that Bremer's father, Adolph, was a close personal friend of President Franklin D. Roosevelt. This brought the gang and the kidnapping into a sharper focus for the FBI, who needed the publicity of a successful arrest in what was becoming an increasingly common crime in a gang-ridden society.

Bremer was kept in captivity for a difficult twenty-two days as a ransom was negotiated. Bremer was a demanding and difficult prisoner, and with little sign of a substantial payout imminent, the situation was fraught. Finally a ransom of $200,000 was agreed on (far less than the gang had planned for), and they wasted no time in releasing a bruised and battered Bremer—a nationwide manhunt then ensued. Karpis and the Barker boys were already public enemies, and Bremer's kidnapping just added to their long list of bank robberies, murders, and extortions.

The gang hoped to implement the perfect crime but made some basic errors that led to their ultimate downfall. Bremer was blindfolded in captivity by a length of gauze material— which, unknown to his captors, was actually see-through, thus giving Bremer the opportunity to locate the hideout. Bremer was able to identify the design of the wallpaper decorating the house, allowing the FBI to trace all wallpaper sales for that particular pattern. This led them to the hideout, which was confirmed by the furniture, picket fences, daily train noises, and familiar neighborhood sounds Bremer recalled from his time in captivity. At the house they discovered a discarded flashlight that was purchased from a local store; the store clerk was then able to identify the gang from their mugshots.

The FBI caught up with Doc Barker in Chicago on January 8, 1935. Upon his arrest the authorities found him in possession of a map that gave the location for his brother and mother. On January 16, government agents shot and killed Freddie Barker and Kate ("Ma") Barker in Florida as they tried to resist arrest; four years later, Doc Barker was himself shot and killed during a failed escape attempt from Alcatraz prison. The FBI arrested the last member of the gang, Alvin Karpis, on May 1, 1936, in New Orleans; he was also incarcerated on Alcatraz.

INVESTIGATION

The Spirit of an Office Worker

Our investigation started in the main offices, where the brewery's financial dealings were scrutinized and organized. We were led through a long corridor where rows of open doors gave us a brief glimpse of dilapidated office furniture strewn about and long-since-redundant paperwork. Two huge walk-in safes decorated this area with ornate, heavy doors and wooden surrounds. At the end of the corridor, at the top of the staircase, sat an old-fashioned telephone switchboard with an empty seat where the operator would have positioned herself or himself.

Tim said he could see the spirit of a woman waiting to connect the calls that were never going to come—the echo of a residual haunting. He said her name was Betty and that she had spent her entire working life *in situ*, connecting the outside world to all parts of the brewery. I recognized the fact that this was the same name as Edward Bremer's daughter and wondered if she had ever been employed by the brewery in later life—but Elizabeth would have been a common name during this period.

A Party of Ghosts

The fine Art Deco staircase opposite the switchboard allowed an opulent descent into the rathskeller (a below-street-level bar or tavern); it was designed by Harry Firminger and is a semiotic embrace of Hollywood and modernist-inspired geometric symmetry. This elegance was in contrast to the giant stuffed buffalo head that greets you above the entrance to the rathskeller. As you walk through the doors you are transported to Bavaria; the room celebrates the Teutonic style in its furniture, fittings, and decoration. The long, solid oak tables that ride the length of the room are overlooked by hunting memorabilia and brewing paraphernalia. A gothic stained-glass window depicting King Gambrinus, the patron saint of beer and hops, casts a Germanic gaze upon our investigation. The hall seemed unnaturally quiet in its retirement, a far cry from the drinking and rowdy celebrations that would have taken place there in its heyday—we started our vigil in the hope of breaking the wake.

We placed a circle of chairs around the front of the great stone fireplace and settled down in the darkness to see who or what would arrive. Slowly, Lisa, Tim, and I noticed a number of spirits coming closer to observe us—curious as to why we were there; Lisa said she could make out five entities on the periphery of our circle. With all investigations I withhold elements of the historical knowledge I have researched from the psychic members of the team; many of the historical facts I uncover have not been previously placed in the public domain.

I asked Tim if he had been given any names for the spirits that had come to see us; he replied that the name *Otto* had come through very clearly and that the one woman in the group had an unusual name beginning with the letter A (that was making it difficult for him to grasp). Otto Bremer, as previously discussed, was the brother of Adolph and the financial guardian of the brewery. I could not find a family connection to the female visitor with the name beginning with A, although I never discovered a comprehensive historical list of all the brewery staff.

The spirits in the room seemed anxious about Lisa's presence (Lisa was the only female member of our team on this vigil); they showed concern that a woman should not be seen in this environment—especially in this male-dominated drinking establishment. They also expressed dissatisfaction with the way we were clothed; we were considered to be poorly attired, and formal dress would have been more appropriate for the grandeur of the hall. I explained that a suit and tie were not the most advantageous attire for the exploration of a dark, disused factory.

The woman with the name beginning with A started to show an interest in my accent and via Tim asked me if England was still the same as she remembered—this was her place of birth before she arrived in America. I assumed she was from a period of history linked to the brewery from the turn of the twentieth century, so I subsequently spoke of events during the later part of the Industrial Revolution and the end of Queen Victoria's reign. I started to talk about the slum areas of the working classes in the East End of London, and she stopped me in mid-sentence. She informed me that she was from a wealthy background and that her large family home was in the country.

During this dialogue we tried to encourage our spectral visitors to move the trigger objects we had set out and to venture closer—so we could document an EMF reading; this they resisted. As the vigil drew to a close (and with no further contact made), we left the circle and proceeded to collect up our equipment. At that moment the K2 EMF meter, which was placed on the seat of an unoccupied chair within our circle, spiked into the red and stayed there for over a minute—as if an entity had sat in the chair.

The K2 meter has a very limited range of around five inches and should give a constant high reading after a baseline reading of zero when the device has not been moved; to leap from no reading to the highest reading of over 20 milligauss (without any other stimulus) would suggest that a large electrical magnetic energy had arrived and then dissipated close to where the meter was positioned. It was agreed that a glass of beer would make an excellent trigger object in this environment, so we poured out a glass and left it on the bar. We made a note of where the level of the beer was and placed the glass on a piece of paper and drew around the base; we then turned off the lights, shut the door, and ventured into the factory.

The Spirit of a Dead Factory Worker

The brewery was vast. Our flashlights beamed into the darkness and faded before they reached the roof or any of the walls. We were informed that if we became separated from our guide we would never find our way out. I thought this to be hyperbole, but after twenty minutes of wandering through random passageways and weaving up and down amongst the many floors and levels, I realized I was wrong.

We moved from the cathedral vastness of some areas into impossibly tight ironwork spiral staircases that led into narrow corridors of intestinal pipe work with wet atmospheres, where our shoulders made contact with both walls; this was claustrophobic and reminiscent of exploring a disused submarine in the dark. Pools of water collected on the floor, and it was reassuring to see our own drying footprints on the way back just to reaffirm that we weren't lost.

As we picked our way through the subterranean gloom, we stopped suddenly. Tim said he could see what looked like a man standing in amongst the industrial dereliction—the man was unwilling to communicate with him other than to tell him psychically that he was a fireman. A speakeasy had existed deep within the unseen recesses of the brewery that had played host to the local police and fire departments during Prohibition. Could a firefighter from the 1920s still be keen to make his way to the illegal alcohol on offer?

It was alleged that Adolph Bremer played fast and loose with the law and that brewing had still taken place on a scaled-down level during this era. A secret club for the law-enforcement officers of the Twin Cities would have certainly facilitated a blind eye—this small, private drinking room had the added comedic convenience of a tap that led directly into one of the vast beer vats.

The brewery had enjoyed a long period of success until Prohibition struck—when the Eighteenth Amendment decreed in 1919 that every brewery in the United States be closed for the production of beer. The brewery was forced then to look towards developing other products; after a failed attempt at manufacturing soft drinks, a nonalcoholic malt beverage was created and became extremely popular. When beer was again legalized in 1933, the Schmidt Brewery found itself to be the seventh-largest brewery in the entire United States; this post-Prohibition growth peaked in 1939, when the production capacity reached 750,000 barrels per annum facilitated by a staff of over five hundred.

After the investigation, with the contact made with the fireman still in my thoughts, I researched to see if any records of an industrial accident existed in the brewery (the chemistry involved in the brewing process can be highly dangerous). I discovered that on October 2, 1896, a huge explosion took place that seriously injured sixteen workers; unfortunately, two of those workers failed to recover and died of their injuries. They were the chief engineer named Edward (no last name given) and the assistant engineer, Otto Keiser. This was a remarkable coincidence when you consider that one of the names that came through in the rathskeller was Otto—could this be the same man who had died in the explosion, and not Otto Bremer as previously thought?

I then started to unearth many more newspaper articles that highlighted the deaths and injuries that had taken place in the brewery—they could all leave a considerable amount of negative energy and paranormal anguish. Two incidents actually happened within months of one another in 1901 and 1902:

Jacob Scroepfer yesterday began a suit in the district court to recover $6,000 damages from the Jacob Schmidt Brewing company for personal injuries, which he claims to have received by an explosion of gas inside a tank where he was at work. The complaint alleges that Scroepfer was set to clean and varnish the inside of the large vats in the defendant's brewery. These were heated, in order that they might receive the coat of varnish, and the accident to which the plaintiff charges his injuries resulted, it is said, from the fact the vat into which he had crawled was overheated. This occurred on Feb. 9, 1901, when Scroepfer carried a can of varnish and a lighted candle into a vat, and the explosion immediately followed. He claims that he was imprisoned in a sheet of flame and severely burned.[61]

Herman C. Kelm, as administrator of the estate of Herman F. Kelm, who was killed by falling through an elevator shaft at the Schmidt Brewery last March, has commenced an action against the Schmidt Brewing Company for $5,000. Kelm was a cooper employed at the brewery. In leaving the room he stepped into an open elevator shaft, falling to the cellar twenty feet below, sustaining injuries which caused his death. The defendant company is charged with negligence in allowing the elevator shaft to remain unguarded.[62]

It was during this research process that I finally unearthed some precious, previously lost information—almost a year after the investigation. I discovered that a brewery worker named Matthew Kohler had died in terrible circumstances in the area where we had engaged with the spirit of the fireman. As I sat in the Minnesota Historical Society reading room, a chill ran down my spine and I trembled, holding the fragile, crisp, yellow newsprint, reading with astonishment that Matthew Kohler was a fireman!

I had naturally believed that the spirit we had made contact with was a fireman in the sense of being a firefighter; Matthew Kohler's job description was also a fireman, but he was responsible for keeping the furnaces fired and for lighting the oil lamps. This article appeared in the *Saint Paul Daily Globe* on April 16, 1904:

Matthew Kohler, a Fireman, is Fatally Injured—Matthew Kohler of 399 Duke Street, while filling a lamp at Schmidt's brewery, on Seventh Street, about 5:30 last evening, was terribly burned and his injuries will prove fatal. Kohler was employed in the engine room as a fireman, and had worked for the brewery for a number of years, and was considered an efficient and industrious worker. Just before dark every evening it was Kohler's duty to draw the fires and see that everything was in shape for the night. Last evening he started to fill on oil lamp, and in doing so spilled some of the oil onto his clothing. In some manner the oil became ignited and in a second he was enveloped in flames. Other employees of the concern who were in the fire room at the time rushed to his assistance and extinguished the flames, but not before Kohler had inhaled them. The city hospital was called and an ambulance was sent to the brewery. At the hospital it was found that the man had been burned from the lower part of the body to the top of the head. The physicians say that his injuries are fatal. Kohler is thirty-seven years of age, and has a wife and six children.[63]

As predicted, this poor man died in the worst possible circumstances:

Fireman Dies From His Burns—Matthew Kohler, the fireman who was terribly burned at Schmidt's brewery Friday evening, died at the city hospital yesterday morning at 9 o'clock. Kohler suffered from inhaling the flames.[64]

What I had achieved in those few sad sentences was a complete vindication of the psychic process—to corroborate information given to me on an investigation some considerable time after the event. Only my own dedication and research skills, applied over hundreds of hours spent searching through dusty old newspapers in dark vaults of historical societies, could have provided me with such information. I now firmly believe, based on this experience, that if I cannot find the historical evidence of a name that is presented to me from the other side, then it is solely because I have yet to find it, and I need to keep looking.

In the lowest, most remote inner belly of the brewery I was perplexed to observe an ever-growing collection of graffiti, with tags sprayed in all manner of colors. As my narrow flashlight beam searched the walls, the crude and naïve nature of the graffiti was revealed and was reminiscent of prehistoric cave art. The factory had been regularly trespassed, and this was the farthest area you could reach within the building; the graffiti showed the sport of leaving a mark as a measure of bravery in making it through the labyrinth and paranormal darkness to this point. We cleared the spent spray cans and settled down to start the second vigil.

The Residual Energy of a Criminal Act

We all sensed that a terrible crime had taken place in this desolate and dystopic environment. Tim got tearful as he started to see the pieces of the picture that was forming—he could see that an assault had taken place. Three men had attacked a woman and it was of a sexual nature; they had dragged her down into this location against her will. Tim focused to see if he could get the name of the woman; he said to the group, "Ruth." A second after him, the ghost box (which up until this point had been unusually quiet) also shouted out the name "Ruth" into the echoing blackness.

We believed this to be a residual haunting, a traumatic event that has become imprinted into the environment, replayed over and over again in the same spot like a video recording. I have found no information relating to a crime of this nature taking place; it is of course possible that Ruth never came forward to report the incident. The factory has only been disused since 2004, and it is believed that a residual haunting tends to be more prominent and vivid the closer it was to the event that took place. We left this area feeling very emotional and upset.

The Power of Protection

We moved across the cobbled street into what was the bottling plant for our final vigil. We made our way through the offices and storerooms: coffee cups were left on desks, telephones were left off the hook—as though a conversation had been suddenly interrupted. Documents were scattered around meeting rooms, and filing cabinets were left open to expose confidential paperwork with staff details. I ventured to open a fridge door and found several moldy lunches that had not felt the waft of fresh air since the factory closed. The locker rooms still had towels hanging on pegs, and odd shoes were liberally scattered around the broken tiled floor.

The place had the feel of a factory whose employees had come to work one day only to find the building locked and no longer operational; this created a very unnerving and uncomfortable sensation, to witness the minutiae of a noisy, bustling center of activity reduced to the now-empty void of nothingness. An overactive imagination could easily be led into believing that this would be the scene that greets you after a nuclear war.

The third vigil provided no evidence of any worth—the lot of a paranormal investigator is to sit for hours on end in the dark with little or nothing happening. I could not help but feel disappointed though, as our expectations were high after our previous experiences around the brewery. As we packed away our equipment and left the location we ventured into an area we had not previously discovered. We found that the bottling building was now being used as a storage space for the city's salt supply, for use on the icy Minnesota roads. I have never seen so much salt in one place; it would not have been unreasonable to entertain the idea of skiing down what was truly a mountain of salt.

It has long been believed that salt has a unique relationship with the paranormal; it is used as a cleansing tool and can be preventative of paranormal activity. I began to wonder if the vast amount of salt in this building was suppressing or removing the activity that was evident in the rest of the brewery. In the Wiccan religion, salt is seen as symbolic of the element Earth and is a purifier of sacred spaces. In Catholic tradition, salt is mandatory in the rite of the Tridentine Mass and is added to water in the Roman Catholic rite of holy water. Salt is also the third item (which includes an exorcism) of the Celtic Consecration (Gallican Rite) that is employed in the consecration of a church.

Paranormal Activity and Water

It is a common perception that paranormal activity tends to be more prevalent in and around water; the brewery evolved on its current site due to the discovery of natural spring water that flows through the caves below. The water is located 1,100 feet beneath the surface and is believed to be more than 30,000 years old. It was created when glaciers bulldozed their way over the river valley during the last ice age; they pushed a vast layer of sediment over the top of the water, creating a pressure that sealed the basin off—a process that stopped the water from seeping out.

This body of water is called the Mt. Simon-Hinckley aquifer; it has been steadily added to by rain water that has spent millennia filtering its way through the rocks and limestone. The water was pumped up from the basin via the deepest drilled holes of any brewery in the United States, straight into the beer-making process, allowing the customers of the Schmidt brewery to be the first to drink the water—albeit in beer—since the woolly mammoth quenched its thirst there (the brewery still sells water to the local population).

The Mystery of the Beer Glass

At the end of our long night of investigating, I remembered the glass of beer we had left out in the rathskeller as a trigger object; Tim and I ventured back to observe our experiment. We could see that the beer had noticeably moved farther down in the glass by at least an inch; the glass, though, had not moved outside of the drawn circle. It could be that one of the spirits we met in this room took advantage of the opportunity to once again taste beer, but my healthy, skeptical side could not help but reason that our guide, the only person with the keys and access to this area, had temptation placed before him as we were making our way around the other parts of the brewery.

CONCLUSION

Beer production came to an end at the Schmidt Brewery in June 2002; the smell of brewing was then temporarily replaced with the bitter stink of ethanol production. The Gopher State Ethanol Company continued to manufacture ethanol for a further two years on the site (this was the nation's first urban ethanol-processing plant), but financial ruin, rather than the pending court battles over the smell and safety, left the building vacant from May 2004 onwards. The significant and idiosyncratic architecture was then recognized when the brewery was placed on a list in 2005 (compiled by the Preservation Alliance) of Minnesota's top ten most-endangered historic places. The future of the brewery remains uncertain, but any future redevelopment of the site for apartments would significantly change the exterior and the interior of the building, destroying a brewing history that spans well over a century. The layer of paranormal activity may be harder to remove though; there could be a time in the future when a resident of a newly built Schmidt Brewery apartment sits up in bed one night to see an ex-worker walking across the room in front of them.

The verification of the mediumship in the factory by historical facts after the event still sends a chill down my spine; the moment I discovered the article relating to the fireman's death was a huge step in the evolution of this book and for the direction it was going to take—it made me realize that paranormal investigating and historical research could sit together in one text and each could inform the other.

Epilogue

This book has been a journey and a culmination of three years' worth of work, during which time I have seen very little daylight—my days have been spent in the vaults of historical societies and my nights spent investigating. There are many more places I still want to investigate in Minnesota though, and other locations I investigated did not make it into this book due to size constraints. As an overview, I found that nearly all of the buildings shared similar traits: a Native American history of the land, people bringing negative energy into the building, similar construction materials, violent or painful deaths connected to the property, the continual energy of people passing through, and an association with water.

The correlation between paranormal activity and flowing water did become a prominent theme throughout my research; a theory for this may come from examining the sedimentary minerals that are found in river beds—like iron pyrite (fool's gold), limestone, and quartz. Iron pyrite is a semiconductor that has an electrical conductivity between that of a conductor and an insulator and is used in the production of modern electronic devices; limestone is made up of chalcedony, flint, and jasper and makes up at least 10 percent of all sediment. Quartz is the second-most abundant mineral in the Earth's crust and has piezoelectric properties; this allows it to develop an electric field or potential upon the application of mechanical stress—so it is good at storing electromagnetic energy.

The flow of water over these minerals could conduct naturally occurring EMF—which emits into its surroundings; it could then be suggested that this energy is stored by the properties inherent in the sediment and discharged like a battery. This would provide ghosts with a source of energy to make manifestations possible or to create physicality (we actually bring electrical magnetic pumps to investigations to create this environment artificially).

The theory of linking water to paranormal activity is not new. Native American cultures believe water to be a gateway where spirits and ghosts—both good and bad—can enter or leave this world. Many locations dotted along the flowing water of the Mississippi are believed in Indian lore to be vortexes. We can see that the Schmidt Brewery, the Soap Factory, the S.S. *William A. Irvin*, the Chase on the Lake resort, and the Mounds Theatre all have an association with water. Interestingly, Mantorville is located on a limestone quarry with an underground spring running through it; the Saloon in Taylors Falls is built on a limestone cave; the Wabasha Street Caves are carved into limestone; and Fort Snelling is constructed entirely from limestone and is surrounded by water on two sides. Farther afield, it is worth mentioning that the mystical Great Pyramids of Giza are also constructed solely from limestone.

I hope I have succeeded in expanding the social history of Minnesota further. Other historians will perhaps come along after me and use this text in a synthesis with other texts to provide further information, or even as an anti-thesis to this thesis (in a Hegelian manner)—but this is how our knowledge and understanding of the past is extended and built upon. I am not here to convince you that paranormal activity exists; you can make your own mind up. All I am doing is presenting a 100 percent factual accounting of the events that have happened to me in an unbiased presentation. During this process I have seen full-bodied apparitions, witnessed violent assaults, spoken in depth with many entities on all manner of subjects, seen objects move, and received corroboration and justification of both my equipment and mediumship.

I was also given information that had been previously lost to the knowledge of man, which subsequently turned out to be true with extensive research after the event. The historical information that I uncovered in many cases cleared up many incorrect facts that were already in the public domain; it proves that we can actually learn diverse history with depth, interest, and insight from the dead—if we just care to listen.

My gratitude and thanks to the following locations:
Minneapolis City Hall
350 S. Fifth Street
Minneapolis, MN 55415

The Palmer House Hotel & Restaurant

500 Sinclair Lewis Avenue
Sauk Centre, MN 56378

Historic Mounds Theatre

1029 Hudson Road
St. Paul, MN 55106

Fort Snelling

Minnesota State Highway 5 and Tower Road
St. Paul, MN 55488

The Soap Factory

514 Second Street SE
Minneapolis, MN 55414

Chase on the Lake

502 Cleveland Blvd.
Walker, MN 56484

S.S. *William A. Irvin*

301 Harbor Drive
Duluth, MN 55802

Mantorville Opera House

55 Fifth Street West
Mantorville, MN 55955

LeDuc Historic Estate

1629 Vermillion Street
Hastings, MN 55033

Wabasha Street Caves

215 Wabasha Street South
St. Paul, MN 55107

The Old Jail Bed & Breakfast

349 W. Government Street
Taylors Falls, MN 55084

The St. James Hotel

406 Main Street
Red Wing, MN 55066

Schmidt Brewery

882 Seventh Street West
St. Paul, MN 55102

Acknowledgments

I'd like to thank all those, deceased and living, who have contributed to and made this historical, paranormal adventure through Minnesota possible.

DECEASED

Monique, Christena Palmer, Edward Barnum, Al Tingley, Ivy Hildebrand, Lucy, Red, Carrie, Jim Dolan, Joe and Victoria, Sarah, Isabel, Edward (keep up the good work), William, Ellen, Frank and Peter Mantor, Cathy, Robert, William, Emma, Harriet, Etta, Charles, Clara, Betty, Otto, Matthew, and Doris.

LIVING

The following supported me, kept me sane, kept me focused, and were there for me in various ways when I needed them: Lisa Lee; my friends and colleagues at The International Paranormal Society past and present—Tim, Ron, Sherry, Erin,

Steve R., Steve H. and Colleen, Lou, Sam, Warren, Kate, Angela, Robin, Heather, Ashley, Cathy and Kevin, Mary, Griffin, Becky, Jo, Diane, Amanda, and Kelly Ann; Kelley and Brett Freese and the staff of the Palmer House Hotel; Jackie and the staff of the Mounds Theatre; the staff and management of Fort Snelling; Jamie and Steve at the Chase on the Lake resort; the Dakota County Historical Society staff and management of the LeDuc Historical Estate; Donna Bremer at the Wabasha Street Caves; Don Lawrence and Kate Holland at the Old Jail Bed & Breakfast; the staff and management at the S.S. *William A. Irvin*—including Brian; Minneapolis City Hall; Scott and the management team at the St. James Hotel; Dave at the Schmidt Brewery; Ben Heywood and his team at the Soap Factory (who do fabulous work: www.soapfactory .org); the good people of Mantorville—including Paul, Melisa, and John; Dave Schrader and the crew of *Darkness Radio* and KTLK-FM; the Luton Paranormal Society—Andy, Elaine, Stephanie, and Bill; Annie Wilder for all her support and help; the Sauk Centre Area Historical Society; Adam Nori, Dan and Greg, Helen, Stephen Easley, Chris Knowles, Dave and Mari T., Lorna, Judi, Jyeton, Eva, Robert, Margaret, Ann, Marlene, Jenn, and Barbara at heavenandearth essentials.com, Mum, Dad, and Joanne (sis)—and the rest know who you are.

All photographs (unless stated on the copyright page) are by Adrian Lee.

Photograph of the author by Meyer's Photography Studio of Sauk Centre (www.meyersphotographystudio.com).

To all the negative spirits and energies out there: I have read to the end of the good book, and we win!

Endnotes

1. "John Moshik Pays the Penalty for Murder." *Saint Paul Daily Globe*, March 18, 1898, p. 1.

2. *Saint Paul Daily Globe.* March 19, 1898, p. 5.

3. "Elevator Is Stuck." *Saint Paul Daily Globe*, April 18, 1905, p. 3.

4. "The Unprofessional Crook." *Saint Paul Daily Globe*, March 1, 1904, p. 4.

5. *Sauk Centre Herald.* September 2, 1869.

6. *Sauk Centre Herald.* June 23, 1870.

7. Hildebrand, Ivy Louise. *Sauk Centre: The Story of a Frontier Town.* Sauk Centre, MN: Sauk Centre Area Historical Society, 1993.

8. *Sauk Centre Herald.* February 20, 1868.

9. *Sauk Centre Herald.* April 30, 1868.

10. "Accident—A Difficult Situation." *Sauk Centre Herald*, May 7, 1868.

11. *Sauk Centre Herald.* April 14, 1870.

12. *Sauk Centre Herald.* June 6, 1870.

13. As quoted in Morgan, Bill. "House Was Slice of Glory for Area." *St. Cloud Times*, February 9, 2006.

14. *Sauk Centre Herald.* September 2, 1869.

15. *Sauk Centre Herald.* February 6, 1868.

16. *Sauk Centre Herald.* February 27, 1867.

17. *Sauk Centre Herald.* March 5, 1868.

18. "St. Paul's Finest Suburban Theater." *Movieland Magazine*, April 1925, p. 15.

19. Blegen, Theodore C. *Building Minnesota.* Boston: D. C. Heath and Company, 1938, p. 84.

20. *Minneapolis Journal.* November 5, 1901, p. 4.

21. *Minneapolis Journal.* October 12, 1901, p. 7.

22. *Saint Paul Daily Globe.* December 31, 1884.

23. "The Soap House Ghost." *Minneapolis Journal*, March 27, 1901.

24. *Saint Paul Daily Globe.* September 6, 1885.

25. Ibid.

26. *Saint Paul Daily Globe.* July 15, 1898.

27. *Saint Paul Daily Globe.* May 18, 1890.

28. *Saint Paul Daily Globe.* November 9, 1881.

29. *Saint Paul Daily Globe.* May 2, 1900.

30. *Minneapolis Journal.* July 20, 1901, p. 15.

31. Ibid.

32. Blegen, *Building Minnesota*, p. 143.

33. "Washington Special: Strange Doings—Some Interesting Developments Relative to Rogers and LeDuc—How Our Paternal President Takes Care of His Friends." *Chicago Times*, January 15, 1878, p. 1.

34. *Saint Paul Daily Globe.* September 7, 1902, p. 14.

35. *Saint Paul Daily Globe.* June 5, 1887, p. 14.

36. "Carey Has a Chance for Life." *Saint Paul Daily Globe*, May 10, 1899. p. 2.

37. *Minneapolis Journal.* May 18, 1901, p. 6.

38. *Minneapolis Journal.* June 18, 1906, p. 18.

39. Blegen, *Building Minnesota*, p. 441.

40. James, Edward T., and Janet Wilson James, eds. *Notable American Women, 1607–1950: A Biographical Dictionary.* Cambridge, MA: Harvard University Press, 1971, p. 151.

41. Bishop, Harriet E. *Floral Home; or, First Years of Minnesota: Early Sketches, Later Settlements, and Further Developments*. New York: Sheldon, Blakeman and Company, 1857. (Republished many times, and it is in the public domain.)

42. Ibid.

43. James and James, eds. *Notable American Women*, p. 151.

44. *Saint Paul Daily Globe*, December 18, 1900, p. 3.

45. *Saint Paul Daily Globe*. September 7, 1883, p. 6.

46. *Saint Paul Daily Globe*, April 1, 1880.

47. *Saint Croix Monitor*, November 1, 1862.

48. As quoted in the *Minneapolis Journal*, December 5, 1902, p. 17.

49. *Taylors Falls Reporter*, March 3, 1871.

50. *Saint Paul Daily Globe*, August 29, 1881.

51. *Saint Paul Daily Globe*, April 6, 1902. p. 10.

52. *Saint Paul Daily Globe*, September 10, 1885, p. 3.

53. Homer. *The Odyssey, with an English Translation by A. T. Murray*. New York: G. P. Putnam's Sons, 1919, p. 397.

54. Homer. *The Iliad*, revised edition. (Translated by E. V. Rieu.) London: Penguin Classics, 2003.

55. *Saint Paul Daily Globe*, May 22, 1878.

56. Ibid.

57. *Saint Paul Daily Globe*, February 23, 1879, p. 1.

58. *Saint Paul Daily Globe*, August 23, 1902. p. 1.

59. "Skull Found." *Sauk Centre Herald*, May 13, 1871.

60. *Saint Paul Daily Globe*, July 12, 1893. p. 2.

61. *Saint Paul Daily Globe*, October 4, 1902.

62. *Saint Paul Daily Globe*, December 24, 1902.

63. "Matthew Kohler, a Fireman, Is Fatally Injured." *Saint Paul Daily Globe*, April 16, 1904, p. 2.

64. "Fireman Dies from His Burns." *Saint Paul Daily Globe*, April 17, 1904, p. 12.